Second-Chance
HORSES

Books by Callie Smith Grant

Second-Chance
HORSES

True Stories of the Horses We Rescue
and the Horses Who Rescue Us

CALLIE SMITH GRANT, ED.

a division of Baker Publishing Group
Grand Rapids, Michigan

© 2023 by Baker Publishing Group

Published by Revell
a division of Baker Publishing Group
Grand Rapids, Michigan
www.revellbooks.com

Printed in the United States of America

Library of Congress Cataloging-in-Publication Data
Names: Grant, Callie Smith, editor.
Title: Second-chance horses : true stories of the horses we rescue and the horses who rescue us / Callie Smith Grant, Ed.
Description: Grand Rapids, Michigan : Revell, a division of Baker Publishing Group, [2023]
Identifiers: LCCN 2022061657 | ISBN 9780800737948 (paperback) | ISBN 9780800745080 (casebound) | ISBN 9781493443512 (ebook)
Subjects: LCSH: Horses—Anecdotes. | Horsemanship—Anecdotes.
Classification: LCC SF301 .S43 2023 | DDC 636.1—dc23/eng/20230215
LC record available at https://lccn.loc.gov/2022061657

Baker Publishing Group publications use paper produced from sustainable forestry practices and post-consumer waste whenever possible.

23   24   25   26   27   28   29   7   6   5   4   3   2   1

To the memory of "Pooh," my horse-crazy sister
who would have loved these stories.

Contents

Contents

A Word to the Reader

My new friend told me that she'd just moved her livestock to a ranch belonging to my brother-in-law. And by livestock, she meant twenty-one miniature donkeys. When I asked her why she had twenty-one miniature donkeys, she looked at me like I was not very bright and said, "Because they're cute."

Fair enough.

"Come see them," she said. "Bring ginger snaps."

The next time I thought about them was during COVID-19 lockdown in 2020. Since we weren't socializing with people face-to-face, I suggested to my husband that we take a drive to the ranch about twenty miles away to find the miniature donkeys—a nice outdoor experience. He was game. I remembered the ginger snaps, so we stopped at a corner store, bought a bag, and off we went.

My brother-in-law had a lot of ranchland on several roads, but try as we might, we could not find those twenty-one little beasts. We never got to feed them ginger snaps. But we humans discovered we like ginger snaps; we ate the whole bag.

You'll meet that friend in this book and learn how she got involved with donkeys in the first place.

There are plenty of horses in these pages, from Arabian stallions to miniature horses to draft horses to Shetland ponies to wild mustangs and everything in between. You'll even meet a zebra.

Yes, a zebra. I've kept my eyes open for a zebra story for years—and this book has it, written by a California equine rescuer who winds up with a beautiful baby zebra. (Did you know that a herd of zebras is called a "dazzle"?)

You'll meet marvelous personalities in the equine world. A new horse on the ranch whose mission seems to be to comfort his human. A donkey who finds his purpose protecting lambs. A pony who somehow figures out how to drive a golf cart. Blind horses who teach their human about courage. An old, lonely horse who falls head over heels in love with a pretty new mare. A horse who helps a little girl get over her fear of riding. And so many more. You'll even meet Elvis in one story!

You'll be introduced to many rescuers, some running rescue ranches and some who fell into rescue by circumstance. You'll meet one young woman who went from waiting tables to rescuing dozens of horses at a time and who continues making a difference in the world of rescue. You'll meet animals who are emotionally rescued by one of their own species. And of course, you'll meet humans who are rescued emotionally by their horse or donkey. So many times, there are surprise relationships. As contributor Barbara Ellin Fox puts it, "It's a big responsibility when a horse chooses a person as his own."

The theme is "second chance," and some examples are right out there. Some are more nuanced. The fact is, there are so many second chances in these stories, I had to limit the number of times we used the words! You'll read a few amazing second chances one could consider miraculous. Whenever I read about that sort of thing, I feel especially privileged.

I know some of you readers are horsemen and horsewomen. Some are ranchers and farmers. Some used to ride as children. But many of you are armchair horse people, not in a position or at a point in life to own and ride. You'll meet people in these pages who found other ways to indulge their love for the equine. You may find yourself thinking about creative ways to be with a horse you always wanted. I'm thinking about that myself after reading these stories.

On my desk as I write this, I have a tiny red ceramic cowboy boot. Or in this case, a cowgirl boot, because it belonged to my horse-crazy sister. We were three years apart in age, and while I loved our horses growing up, she completely adored them. Each night after supper when the weather was warm enough, she took her homework to the barn and sat in the hay with her favorite horse and our occasional ponies. They even whinnied outside her bedroom window in the mornings to wake her up.

My sister passed away a few years ago, and while I was at her house shortly afterward, I saw the little red ceramic boot. I picked it up and pocketed it. I keep it as a symbol of the inspiring childhood we had involving animals. She is one of the reasons I started writing about them.

I wish my sister were here to read these stories. I often wanted to call her and talk to her about what I was reading. She loved everything I wrote, as a good big sister would, but she especially loved these collections of stories by others.

So I offer *Second-Chance Horses* to you in her memory. Enjoy the ride!

1

Pumpkin Patch

Andi Lehman

When we fulfilled our daughter's dream of a pony for her eleventh birthday, my husband and I assumed we were "one and done." But, as all horse owners learn, it's hard to have a single equine. Within weeks of our mare's arrival, we received offers for various pals to keep her company. A couple of candidates came and went. And then, we met Pumpkin.

A miniature orange and white paint with a history of hoof disease called founder, Pumpkin needed a new home. He was a fat four-year-old gelding—the equivalent of an overweight preschooler with a chronic eating issue. His busy owner offered him to us for free if we would address the founder and give him the attention she could not.

We drove across the county on a bright winter day to see him, and he was oh-so-cute. His thick, two-colored tail swept the ground as he quickstepped along the fence line, regarding us with one big blue eye and one brown. We laughed at his high-pitched whinny, more of a shrill squeal than a neigh.

A half-horse, as our daughter dubbed him, Pumpkin seemed docile enough, and he was certainly short if not svelte. Her pony would enjoy the companionship, and we would give Pumpkin a good life. How much trouble could a plump mini horse be?

We soon found out. He may have stood only forty inches high, but his diminutive frame housed the heart of a Percheron stallion. While he gave due deference to the lead mare in their herd of two, he set out to be the ruling monarch of us all.

Not that my besotted husband minded. Just looking at Pumpkin transported my spouse back to summer visits on his aunt's farm in Maryland where she raised Chincoteague ponies. He phoned his parents, asking them to send a small saddle.

And he gave Pumpkin a nickname: "The Prince of the Meadow." Each morning before work, he walked to the barn with a carrot to say hello. He roughed up Pumpkin's mane, rubbed his withers, and leaned over to whisper "You're the Prince" in his ear. (I always thought the name "Loki," after the wily Norse god of mayhem, would be more appropriate. In public, I referred to Pumpkin as our yard art—attractive but useless.)

I realized early on that Pumpkin believed minis were not meant for riding. Or showing. Or even leading. Minis exist to do whatever they want and to make people smile, nothing more. They eat, sleep, and play—not necessarily with us.

Our first attempt to saddle Pumpkin also became our last. We thought he would enjoy giving a ride to our seven-year-old son, who weighed less than a meager fifty pounds. It was a toss-up as to who was less enthused, mini-man or mini-mount.

Pumpkin hopped and bucked and tried to shake the saddle off his back, so we should not have been surprised when he did the same with our son. The boy lasted all of five seconds atop the tiny steed, and we never got him on a horse again. To this day, he enjoys them from a distance.

Pumpkin's favorite pastime (other than eating) was scratching his itches on our hog-wire fence. The six-inch-square wire openings functioned as a multi-broad-handed masseuse. Pumpkin scraped his head and neck or his shoulders and flanks against the taut wires, but he especially relished wagging his wide rump back and forth across them like a fat windshield wiper.

In the spring, the wire holes also acted as defoliators for his thick winter coat. Pumpkin spread his shedding self all along our fence line, much to the delight of the birds who lined their nests with his soft fur and long strands from his tail. While I fretted over the unsightly orange and white explosions of horsehair that hugged our property, my daughter and husband just chuckled and called each gift a "Pumpkin patch."

The scamp's innate curiosity and overconfidence got him into repeated trouble. One balmy afternoon while we focused our attention on fence post repairs, Pumpkin ambled over to the electric golf cart we used for hauling our supplies. A bit of snooping led to stepping—right up onto the floor of the vehicle where he somehow hit the gas pedal with his front feet.

We looked up in time to see our fearless mini gazing over the wheel of the golf cart and driving straight toward a section of fence. Helpless, we watched him slam into the wire and squirt out the side of the cart on impact. He took a quick look around, shook himself off, and returned to grazing—clearly hoping there were no witnesses.

Whenever a gate was left open (or was opened by the imp of mischief), our pair of prancers skipped out of their four-acre haven and roamed down the cove, visiting one green lawn after another. That first summer, the visits were so frequent that our neighbors set up a phone relay. We exchanged numbers, and helpful spotters called around to indicate the direction the horses were heading. By the fall, we knew every homeowner in our subdivision.

On his way down our lane, Pumpkin liked to stop at my bird feeders for a quick snack of seeds and fruit. Our first indicator of an equine breakout often came from a glance out the kitchen window. Broken feeders hanging at odd angles or strewn across the lawn usually meant a horse hunt unless we could catch him in the act before he bolted.

When he wasn't marauding, Pumpkin enjoyed the sunflowers I planted on the west side of the barn in the dry lot—he ate them down to nubs. He also snatched big mouthfuls of my mums any time he was led past them from the barn to the round corral. His position of choice seemed to be head-down with jaws working.

We quickly realized we would need to invest in the same kind of training for The Prince that we were giving our pony: expensive and time-consuming but successful. Without it, we'd own a well-behaved adult and an ill-mannered juvenile delinquent. Our talented daughter put her natural horsemanship education to work on her second student.

First, she introduced some basic social skills like respecting her space and yielding to pressure. As soon as Pumpkin could follow her lead consistently, she treated him like a big herding dog and gave him jobs. Once he realized a horse treat might be the payoff for his chores, he followed her around like a puppy.

She filled a burlap feed sack with empty cans and taught her mouthy mini to fetch. Soon he retrieved anything we threw out in the dry lot: the sack of cans, a ball cap, a glove. He even learned to bring in the hard rubber feed bins after each feeding. After carrying them one at a time between his teeth, he released the prize to one of her hands—so long as he spied his treat in the other.

In addition, Pumpkin learned to put his front feet on a pedestal (benefitting, no doubt, from his experience with the golf cart) and to hop atop the wooden plinth on all fours and pose for a photo. Using a twenty-two-foot lead rope, his savvy trainer convinced him to jump the logs we scattered in the meadow, even though he preferred to walk along the tops of them like a sure-footed billy goat on a balance beam.

Unfortunately, we were less successful at getting him to give up grass. While our pony came running at her owner's first whistle, Pumpkin acted like he didn't even hear her. He pushed his face deeper into the green carpet and grazed away at the sweet, sugary blades. Our grass hound's founder problems went from bad to worse. We tried one farrier and then another. We learned there are multiple schools of thought to treating founder, and we dabbled in all of them. Finally, our favorite farrier told us we would never solve the hoof problem until we addressed the food problem by banning The Prince from the meadow.

We set up a lightweight electric wire enclosure inside our big dry lot. But the grass sirens still called to Pumpkin. As winter brought cold temperatures and a thick protective coat to our mini, he simply ducked underneath the wire and accepted the brief sizzle on his back and neck as the price to enter the pasture.

We added a second lower strand to keep him from scooting underneath the first. Clever Pumpkin started testing the fence to see if it was on. Approaching the two strands with due respect, he listened for the faint humming noise from the current. If he didn't hear it, he stretched out his neck to touch the wire with his nose. No shock, no fence. He plowed it down without apology.

Despite our diligent attempts to keep him on a strict diet and off the grass, we didn't see immediate results. So we congratulated ourselves when Pumpkin started to slim down—until he kept losing weight, a lot of it. His movements became uncoordinated, and he had no strength in his hind legs. He walked with an odd wobble, if he walked at all, and he held his neck bowed inward and his feet splayed outward trying to maintain his equilibrium.

Our vet said nothing while he examined Pumpkin. The symptoms pointed to EPM, equine protozoal myeloencephalitis, a degenerative neurological disease spread by the saliva or feces of wild opossums. The prognosis wasn't good, and at this stage of the illness, the doctor gave Pumpkin a 50/50 chance of survival. He left us a special powder and a paste to administer faithfully, which our daughter did for weeks. Her dad visited the patient daily to offer a rub of encouragement or a carrot, which Pumpkin refused—a sure sign of his distress. We missed the sound of his quick-trotting steps and his wee whinnies. We worried and prayed.

But time and attention and the wise council of our vet and farrier won out. And some unexpected benefits came from the ordeal. After Pumpkin was forced to rest and eat only what he was fed, his hooves grew back to nearly normal as he got stronger. And he never regained all his previous weight, which left him healthier than he had been prior to his sickness.

Post EPM, the close bond between my husband and my daughter deepened as they shared their joy in The Prince's recovery. They took impromptu pictures of our brave survivor and texted them to each other. The horse's name appeared painted on a large board above his stall. Orange pumpkin cutouts decorated the walls, high enough to be unreachable by small inquisitive teeth.

My doting spouse gave our firstborn a six-inch Schleich model horse that looked just like Pumpkin, and the figure started popping up in all kinds of places inside our house as they took turns hiding and finding the toy. Soon my son and I joined the game we called "Where's Pumpkin?" Whoever found him hid him next. That Christmas our daughter made her dad a hardback book of the same name filled with photos of all the locations "little Pumpkin" had visited during the year.

Not to be outdone, the real Pumpkin also invaded our house. His resident trainer decided to see if she could get him to approach and enter through the back door. Standing to one side of him, she raised the lead rope toward the open doorway and exerted slight pressure forward. He ambled across the threshold, walked through the foyer into the kitchen, and looked around with interest as if he might join us for breakfast. We gave him some treats and took a snapshot for our fridge, where his royal visage could greet us every morning.

While one of our children was building her life around horses, the other built his in the theater. And before long, the two intersected. When the local high school teacher who cast our son as Will Parker in *Oklahoma* needed a barnyard scene in her lobby, she asked our family to create an interactive display with animals. We built a life-size barn wall next to the ticket booth and got permission to fence in a square section of tiled floor and fill it with hay—and Pumpkin.

Rabbits, chickens, and a rooster peered at him from their cages along one side of the pen. Our cheerful mini rested his chin on the wooden rails and accepted as his right the pats of hundreds of patrons throughout five public performances. At the end of the theater season, we brought home three coveted regional awards, including one for Best Lobby Design.

Years later, Pumpkin made another house call during the first summer we faced the monster COVID. My favorite clients at the First Regional Library system asked me to give educational presentations with my animal partners in a live Zoom format since we couldn't meet as we usually did on-site at the individual branches.

The summer library reading theme was Fables and Fairy Tales, and I titled my opening Zoom program "Princes, Princesses, and Ponies." I asked my daughter for footage of her horses, who had multiplied again and now numbered four. She created a magical PowerPoint for me highlighting their unique traits and explaining to viewers why each one reminded her of a different Walt Disney steed.

She showed several engaging videos of her equine friends, and we crowned the hour-long program with our live surprise guest, Pumpkin. He sailed through the familiar back door, stepped onto the blankets we spread along his path "just in case," clopped through the kitchen, the den, and down a hall past three bedrooms to enter my office. Once he arrived, he blew out a whuffle of air and waited, gently swishing his magnificent tail and stretching his nose toward the camera. We tossed a ball cap on the carpet, and he did his best retriever imitation a few times (for a horse treat, of course). He stayed and visited for about ten minutes before returning the way he came—no fuss, no attitude, no accidents. First a thespian and now a movie actor, The Prince proved what he already knew—he was the star, the reigning monarch.

Today, at twenty-two, Pumpkin still rules the barnyard. Our daughter likes to say she owns three and a half horses. But what a half! He rears up on stout little legs to nip the necks of both my daughter's big geldings and delights in dodging around their legs, trying to agitate them into play.

He also resides in a stall with the old blind mare who first welcomed him to her meadow. He serves her now as a stalwart partner, sharing her hay manger, giving her grace when she bumps into him, and protecting her from the horse in the stall next to them by administering a swift bite if the usurper threatens his pony pal.

For a little horse who has never been shown, never competed in a horse event, and never been ridden (for long), Pumpkin has added colorful and unexpected threads to the patchwork quilt of our family story. Sometimes a rescued animal fills our lives in places we didn't even know were empty.

Pumpkin did.

2

Once-in-a-Lifetime Horse

DeVonna R. Allison

As soon as I saw Geronimo prancing inside a round pen, I knew he was special. A deep red-over-white paint quarter horse, he was flashy, yes, but there was something else about him. Geronimo had "presence."

Though past his prime and retired from the rodeo circuit, Geronimo still moved like an athlete. His head held high, his intelligent eyes watched the barnyard, noticing everything. His nostrils drank in every scent. He continued to prance around his enclosure as I crossed the gravel drive and my breath caught in my throat. This horse was breathtaking.

Geronimo wasn't my first horse. Horses are expensive pets; it's worth it to take time before buying one. Besides the costs of feeding a 1,200-pound animal, horses require regular farrier visits to maintain their feet and hooves. Naturally there will also be occasional vet bills, monthly worming, annual shots, and disease testing. Buying Geronimo was a decision I did not take lightly.

The rancher handling the sale stepped into the round pen and caught Geronimo easily and held him for me. The horse's hooves were neatly trimmed and his feet sound. He had a friendly, approachable demeanor, and his teeth were appropriate for his age.

He was not head-shy. He backed willingly and responded readily to whatever was asked of him. He was saddled, and my son mounted, steering him toward a sand exercise ring just beyond the stable.

"Be careful to avoid the barrels," the rancher cautioned, pointing at the opposite end of the ring; Geronimo was a trained barrel racer. The horse went smoothly through his paces, and when my son reined up at the side of the ring, I ran my hand down Geronimo's warm, satiny side.

"I'll take him," I said.

Shaking hands, the rancher and I agreed upon a price and day of delivery. That magnificent horse was mine! As we walked back to our truck, my heart sang. *Thank you, Lord! He's just what I was looking for!*

I had no idea he would be so much more.

Four years earlier, our family had embarked on a new adventure when we bought our dream home on five acres. We received the keys on the first day of June and prepared for the move. The house and land had been neglected for several years, so there was a lot to do. Rolling up our sleeves, we dove into the work as a family. It was truly a labor of love.

On the 25th of June that year, our oldest son, Wesley, was invited to a sleepover by his best friend. Wes was fourteen and a huge help—as were his three younger siblings—with all the work on the new property. That week, Wes and my husband, Earl, had ripped out all the old carpeting; it was a dusty, stinky, sweaty job. Wes deserved some fun.

I kissed Wes goodbye at 3:30 in the afternoon. At a little after 6:00 that same evening, we got the call that rocked our world. Wesley had drowned.

The next month and a half are a blur in my memory. The funeral was large, standing-room only, and people were kind. But their lives quickly went back to normal afterward. Ours did not.

We finally got moved into the new house in the middle of August. We settled in, ordered new carpeting, painted, and tried to figure out how to be a family of five when once we'd been six. We limped along, leaning heavily on our faith and one another.

23

Some days were better than others, but gradually our lives took on a new rhythm.

Dealing with their own grief, our three surviving children were soon caught up in school, sports, friends, and 4-H. Earl returned to his job and found some solace in his work. A stay-at-home mom, I took a small part-time job, continued to care for my family, and struggled with the yawning inner void left by my son's death.

The week before I first saw Geronimo, I joined Earl outside our barn. Dusk settled in, filled with typical country-night sounds. Frogs, cicadas, and crickets sang their summer evening melodies, and our roosting chickens purred and chuckled in the henhouse. I swatted the occasional mosquito, watching Earl load his truck with tools and equipment for the following day's work.

"I wish I could just find something to help, you know?" I said. "Nothing seems to take my mind off this terrible . . ." I stopped. The words caught in my throat, and tears welled up. Earl paused and came to me in the gathering darkness. We held each other.

"I know," he said. "I know."

Our moment was interrupted by the phone ringing in the house. I ran to answer it, wiping my eyes as I went. It was our neighbor, Linda, from a half a mile down the road.

"Hey, DeVonna," Linda greeted me. "I know it's been a while since you mentioned it, but are you still looking for a horse? I have a friend who can't afford to keep hers any longer. She asked me if I knew of anyone who might be interested in him, and you're the first person I thought of." I'd almost forgotten that conversation. It must have been over six months ago.

"Sure." I shrugged. "I'll take a drive over and look at him. What's the address?"

Of course, I fell in love with the horse.

The day of Geronimo's arrival dawned with clear blue skies. A warm Midwestern sun shone brightly over the deep green corn and soybean fields of high summer. Songbirds flitted back and forth to the feeder outside our picture window, and my flower beds spilled over with blooms. All of this was lost on me as I waited for

Geronimo to be delivered. I was a wreck of nervous anticipation, pacing and peering through the windows toward the drive.

Earl was at work, and the kids were busy with their own pursuits, so I waited alone, fighting the urge to call the rancher. *He is a very busy man,* I reminded myself, *plus he's doing me a big favor by delivering the horse. I will not bug that poor man just because I can't control myself!*

I tried to do some laundry. I say "tried" because after the machine stopped, I realized I hadn't added any detergent. Sighing, I reset the machine and washed the load again, this time with soap. I continued to watch the clock.

Morning faded into early afternoon, and I was considering walking down the drive to check the mail, when . . . hark! Our two dogs shot up from where they lounged on the floor. They stared out the window in silence for a moment, then broke out in excited barking.

A long, gleaming horse trailer appeared at the curve in our driveway. It was quite a rig. Outfits like that could carry up to four stalled horses at a time and had an inside tack room plus sleeping quarters for its riders. It was the Cadillac of horse trailers. The fact that it was pulled by a faded and dusty, work-weary diesel pickup may have struck me as funny any other time. Today I was focused on only one thing. My horse was in there; Geronimo had arrived.

I raced outside where our pony, Poker, whirled and bucked around his pen. Excited by the arrival of this strange vehicle, Poker abruptly slid to a stop. Mane and forelock tossing wildly, he lifted his head, wild-eyed, and sniffed. He'd caught Geronimo's scent. Snorting, the pony stamped both front feet and issued a high and raspy challenging whinny.

Who are you? Poker demanded. *And what are you doing here on my turf?*

From deep inside the gleaming trailer, Geronimo's voice answered, loud, low, and regal. Poker was entranced. He and Geronimo continued to call back and forth to one another, softer now, "talking" together in friendly tones.

I realized I was holding my breath. Exhaling deeply, I waited for the rancher to exit his truck. We greeted one another, and I watched as he lowered the trailer's ramp, swung wide its doors, and then made his way deep inside. I could hear his voice, indistinctly, speaking to Geronimo, the metallic clang of a latch and a chain rattling. Poker and I stood, both of us quivering in anticipation, waiting for them to emerge.

I was afraid I'd exaggerated Geronimo in my memory. I'd only seen him once, and that was a week ago. But the second I saw him that day, I was again taken by his beauty and grace. Stepping daintily down the ramp, he unloaded like a dream. The rancher led him to me, snapped my lead to Geronimo's halter, and handed me the rope. He was officially mine!

Geronimo and I stood together in the leafy shade of our oak tree after the rancher left. The sound of cicadas buzzing hung in the air and mingled with the drifting dust cloud where the truck had passed. Bored again, the dogs returned to the porch, where they lazed beneath my hanging ferns. Geronimo looked around the shady green lawn, taking in the sight of the horse pen, chicken house, barn, and deep north woods. Having seen enough, he dropped his head and began to crop grass, ripping mouthfuls from the lawn.

I couldn't contain my emotions any longer. Throwing my arms around his neck, I leaned against his broad shoulder and wept tears of grief mixed with indescribable joy. I cried harder than I'd allowed myself in a while. Geronimo stood calm and raised his head. I was afraid my outburst would startle him, but he continued chewing a mouthful of grass. His ears flickered back toward the sound of my sobs; his breathing was relaxed and regular. From all appearances, comforting damsels in distress was just part of his job.

The rhythm of my days changed after Geronimo arrived. I climbed out of bed willingly each morning and rushed through my breakfast, eager to be greeted by Geronimo's soft chuckle. I relished caring for him, brushing him, feeding him, leading him to and from the pasture. I discovered his favorite scratching place was just behind his left front elbow. While I scratched, he stood still, closed his eyes, and sighed. I bought him a fancy show halter, which was ridiculously expensive, and a good secondhand Western saddle. I spoiled him with peppermint treats, apple slices, and carrots. I spent hours soaping and polishing his saddle and bridle, my fingers turning wrinkled.

Earl and our son built Geronimo a pen separate from the pony. (Geronimo was greedy with the grain.) The favorite part of my days became the afternoons in the lengthening sunlight when I sat with him. Enjoying his horsey scent, I watched him doze, his tail swishing away flies, his ears back, one hind foot cocked in quiet relaxation.

Our best times, though, were when we rode. Whether we rode down our dirt lane, traveled our country road, or explored the woods together, Geronimo was always an eager, trusting, reliable mount. We often rode past neighboring farms. He was not afraid of traffic.

I began to learn Geronimo's likes and dislikes. For instance, while sheep didn't bother him, he did not like hogs. Near a hog pen he would stop, ears up, feet planted wide, sniffing the scary squealing pigs. I was careful to avoid farms with pigpens near the road.

The huge combines farmers drove through the fields harvesting grain made him nervous. Their large diesel engines roared and put out thick black smoke. The combines rattled and groaned and clanked as they bounced down the asphalt. If we saw one parked quietly in a field, I would stop and let Geronimo sniff and stare for a minute until he relaxed and we continued on our way.

I learned he was not afraid of dogs. On our first ride, a neighbor's slavering, baying Great Dane bounded up to us. I gathered the reins, preparing myself for Geronimo to kick or rear or buck or run. He did none of these. He glanced at the dog without breaking stride and then ignored it, continuing our ride. I wanted to hug him, then and there.

The inexpressible solace of a companionable ride cannot be overstated. One such ride stands out in my memory.

Arriving home from a demoralizing day at work, I pulled up to the mailbox, removed some mail I didn't want to see, and shivered.

The autumn day was damp and chilly with low-hanging, rain-heavy clouds. The gloomy skies matched my mood. I was glad to be home.

Up at the house I checked on the horses. Geronimo greeted me at the gate, ears forward, head up, nickering low and soft, expectantly. I smiled in spite of myself.

"What are you begging for, you big, spoiled boy?" I teased while caressing his velvet nose and lips. He responded by raising a front hoof and tapping the wooden gate sharply. This was his way of asking for a ride. I felt inspired; why not?

I tossed the mail unopened on the desk and headed to the bedroom to change. By the time I reached the bedroom doorway, I was peeling off my office clothes and pulling on my jeans, a long-sleeved tee, and one of Earl's soft flannel shirts. I grabbed my leather boots and a jacket by the back door and headed to the barn. The barn never fails to console me. Its sweet smell of grains and hay mixed with the scents of animal sweat, saddle soap, and leather is an intoxicant that both relaxes and invigorates me.

As Geronimo paced around his pen, his anticipation mirrored my own. I led him out of his pen while he kept his gaze on the path to the open fields. I brushed him and cleaned his feet before smoothing on the saddle blanket and pad. I slung the heavy saddle up and settled it onto his back. Cinching the belly strap, I felt my excitement rise. *I deserve this ride*, I thought. *We both do.*

Mounting, I felt the knots of anxiety in my body ease as I settled comfortably into the saddle and reined Geronimo toward the field. He stepped out briskly, and I took in the sights, sounds, and smells of the woods we passed. The ferns were gone, having turned golden brown after the first frost, and many of the songbirds had migrated, leaving the squirrels to gather and hoard their stores of nuts, alone. Leaves had changed and fallen, destined to become mounds of mulch beneath the trees. The woods looked devoid of life, leafless and birdless, but they also emitted a vibrant and pleasing scent of rich, damp earth and foliage decay.

When I reached the end of the driveway, I could see what had caught Geronimo's eye. A flock of wild Canada geese was gleaning the freshly harvested field. These flocks are such a common sight in our area I'd barely noticed them earlier. I wondered how the geese would react to sharing their field with us. I expected them to scatter and fly away. I was surprised to see them move calmly aside as we passed among them.

Geronimo's attention shifted from the geese to the far edge of the field. I urged him into a trot. In his excitement he moved to canter; Geronimo was eager to run. I knew if I let him dictate our pace, he'd be hard to control, so I brought him back down into a warm-up trot. Geronimo telegraphed his frustration by swinging his head wildly up and down and prancing. I couldn't help but grin at his antics. Snorting and arching his neck, he drew in the sweet, damp smell of the field beneath the low, gray skies.

"Settle down," I soothed him. Leaning forward, I patted his neck. "That's a good boy." His ears swiveled back, listening. He walked smartly on.

Reaching the far end of the field, I clicked my tongue several times, and Geronimo eased into his lovely rocking canter. The cool air, the damp field, the wide, open space—I felt my spirit lift, cleansed. The geese again parted like Moses's sea when we reached them, allowing us to pass among them. We turned. I tested the saddle and leaned forward while squeezing my legs and raising the reins.

"Get up, Geron! Get up!" I urged. He needed no further encouragement.

Swept by the wind of our speed, Geronimo's mane whipped at my face as we flew across the ground, hooves thudding. Together we leaned forward, taking joy in Geronimo's love of movement, his raw power, and our synergy. Rippling laughter of pure joy erupted from my lips, and the geese, hearing the sound, stood tall and broke into a wild symphony of honking.

That night when my family got home, Earl asked about my day. All the terrible parts forgotten, I smiled and said, "I rode through a field of wild geese."

Horsemen will tell you that there is a phenomenon known as the once-in-a-lifetime horse. Such an animal comes around very rarely and occurs when a rider encounters a horse with whom they share a connection so special it seems that horse and rider can almost read each other's minds. Together, horse and rider form a unique bond and understanding that is hard to explain.

Geronimo was my once-in-a-lifetime horse. He came to me at a desperate time in my life, and by being simply who he was, sweet, wise, intelligent, trusting, he comforted me. I believe God used Geronimo to lift me up and out of my darkest time and to allow me to experience again the joys of life and living.

3

Freedom for Sundance

Debbie Garcia-Bengochea

Life can change in an instant, but sometimes it takes a long time for that instant to come.

When I first met little Sundance, the mini horse had been living alone inside a muddy chicken coop since he was a foal. His shaggy tan coat was dirty, his hooves needed to be trimmed, and he nervously paced back and forth in the limited space behind the chicken wire. I was thankful that I had been contacted about his situation and might be able to help.

Horses are highly social herd animals. A normal healthy horse would never live alone by choice. They want companionship and are happier and healthier if they can run and play with their own kind. A lonely horse can never relax or feel safe.

The instant Sundance looked at me with his huge brown eyes, I knew I could not let him stay one more day in the old chicken coop. Even though his life up until that moment had been one of loneliness and poor care, his eyes still seemed kind and trusting. He stepped out of the chicken coop with a halter on for the first time, sniffed the ground, and nibbled on a blade of grass. With the help of some treats and reassuring scratches, he walked up the ramp of our horse trailer and into his new life.

When Sundance arrived at our farm, he had to stay isolated from the other horses until we knew more about his health and had administered much-needed care. From his paddock he could see his future equine friends galloping together in the distance. Sundance whinnied to them, and the horses whinnied back. They were the first horses he had seen since he was a baby.

The herd Sundance saw running together were Gentle Carousel Miniature Therapy Horses. For the last twenty-five years, tiny horses from our nonprofit charity have visited thousands of patients in children's and veterans' hospitals across the country. They were called in to comfort survivors and first responders during the tragedies at Sandy Hook Elementary School in Newtown, Connecticut, the Emanuel African Methodist Episcopal Church in Charleston, South Carolina, and the Pulse nightclub in Orlando, Florida. They helped the tornado survivors of Moore, Oklahoma, victims of the fires in Gatlinburg, Tennessee, families in the aftermath of Hurricane Irma, and families and first responders after the condo collapse in Surfside, Florida.

Once Sundance's hooves mended and his health improved, he was finally able to meet some of the horses up close. He was so excited. I decided to introduce him to sweet therapy horses Sparkle and Circus.

We gave Sundance a chance to smell and see Sparkle and Circus from a distance on the first day. On the second day they greeted each other from opposite sides of a fence in neighboring paddocks. Sundance was able to interact with his new friends for short periods of time over the course of several days. Gradually we lengthened the amount of time they spent next to each other. Finally, the new friends were released together in Sundance's paddock.

When horses meet each other for the first time, they usually stand nose to nose, breathing into each other's nostrils. It is a horse hello. Sparkle and Circus stayed calm while Sundance ran around them for a few minutes, then came over to sniff their noses. They gently blew back a friendly greeting.

Everything was new to Sundance at his new home, but over time he learned to imitate Sparkle and Circus. When I called them, he followed along to enjoy hugs and neck rubs. When I walked them on lead lines, he learned to join them. Even challenges like calmly taking a bath or having his feet lifted for regular hoof trims were easier with friends nearby.

Sundance loved to buck and race around his paddock. Every day was a new day of freedom. He also enjoyed exercising with Sparkle and Circus in our round training arena. The faster he could run, the happier he seemed to be. It was a wonderful day when he was finally able to join Sparkle and Circus with his forever herd of companions as they galloped across many acres together.

Sparkle and Circus started training to become therapy horses when they were foals and already had spent many years visiting children inside hospitals. They also worked with Gentle Carousel's literacy programs and book festivals for young and at-risk readers.

The horses of Gentle Carousel go through a two-year basic in-hospital training program, but they are always learning new skills. The therapy horses work with medical professionals in oncology units and in the ICU and with occupational, speech, and physical therapists as part of the treatment for patients who have suffered strokes, traumatic brain and spinal cord injuries, amputations, and burns.

Safely traversing high-rise hospital buildings would be a challenge for any horse, but Sparkle and Circus make it look easy. These therapy horses walk up and down steps, ride in elevators, walk on unusual floor surfaces, carefully move around hospital and television studio equipment, work in small patient rooms, and stay calm around unexpected sounds like ambulances, alarms, and hospital helicopters. And yes, they are house trained.

Miniature horses may be small, but they are normal horses in every way. It takes a special horse, no matter the size, to be both safe and happy working indoors. Not every job is right for every horse. Unlike therapy dogs, horses evolved as prey animals, and their first response to anything scary is flight. Would Sundance be able to join his friends visiting patients or comforting families facing challenges? Was he a horse who could overcome his past and be relaxed and careful around small children, no matter what was going on around him?

The answer was yes! Even though his first years of life had been difficult, Sundance still had a beautiful tenderness, especially with children. With time, love, and lots of practice, Sundance now visits young hospital patients and is an important member of Gentle Carousel's literacy programs. He often joins other therapy horses and teams of volunteer professional educators to inspire young readers. Sundance works inside schools and libraries, with mentoring programs, at children's book festivals, and at educational resource centers in high crime neighborhoods with a focus on at-risk readers.

Many of our individual therapy horses have been featured as characters in children's books by different authors and publishers. After a story is read to children, the actual character from the book comes out to meet them and bring the book to life. Sundance was asked to be a character in a book about children living in foster care. He even learned to kiss his photo on a page as an autograph. Over the years Sundance has encouraged hundreds of wonderful young friends as they wait for their own forever families.

Sundance, the little horse who lived in a tiny chicken coop, now runs free with a lifelong herd. Circus and Sparkle remain Sundance's favorite horses to spend time with. I often see them grazing together or enjoying the shade of a tree on a sleepy afternoon. Sometimes they travel together, bringing their special love to those who need it most. Therapy horses at Gentle Carousel work no more than two days a week, so Sundance always has plenty of time to enjoy his freedom and his best friends—and to make a difference in so many lives.

A Horse of Her Own

Jenny Lynn Keller

As far back as I remember, two world events occur the first week in May—the Kentucky Derby and my sister's birthday. Some years they happen on the same date. One of those years we attended the derby to celebrate her birthday. Although the occasion tests my memory, lots of Thoroughbreds and fancy hats come to mind, along with the monotonous voice of the announcer calling race after race. We waited all day for the premier event, and I don't remember which horse won. But my story is about another horse winning an entirely different type of prize, an award worth more than any horse won that day at the Kentucky Derby.

You see, on the way home the next day, my sister announced she wanted a horse of her own. She emphasized the words "my own" rather loudly from the car's back seat, as if my parents needed to know their significance. Years earlier when she and I were small children, we saved our money earned from doing house chores to buy a horse. The following Christmas we received a Shetland pony for our efforts, and we shared the pinto until we outgrew him. With my sister now on the cusp of becoming a teenager, I reckon she felt quite confident in speaking her mind, although it seemed to me nothing had stopped her previously. As an eyewitness to her

35

whims and antics over the years, I also felt confident her demands would not be met.

A horse requires a considerable amount of daily care, and my sister's approach to life centered around fun. As the life of every party, she preferred activities she enjoyed and ranked necessities like completing homework and house chores low on her priority list. With her track record, I placed a huge bet on my parents telling her no. End of conversation. Good try by the blond-haired, blue-eyed tornado many in our family affectionately called Sarge. Yes, she could be a tad bossy at times.

Guess what? A month later my father introduced us to Frisky, my sister's very own horse. Since I can't recall who registered more surprise that afternoon—me or her—I'm claiming the most shock. Had our parents suddenly gone soft with their rules about us doing our chores? Were they experiencing a midlife identity crisis a few years early? Or worse, did creatures from outer space zap their memories clean? If so, perhaps I should take advantage of their current generous mindset and ask them for a car. Hmm, a thought to ponder. Within weeks I would meet the requirements to obtain my learner's permit.

But my astonishment turned to joy as Sarge rubbed Frisky's shiny brown coat and stroked his forehead accented with a white, irregularly shaped star. He nuzzled her cheek, sniffed her hair, and rearranged its style with a snort. The two shared an instant connection, putting a heartwarming smile on her face and what I labeled a horse grin on his lips. A few apple slices offered as a treat sealed the deal. Frisky and Sarge became best buddies. My father's selection of a quarter horse helped to cement the relationship. Known to be a calm and good-natured breed, quarter horses make ideal companions for young or inexperienced riders. Except for sporadic rides on friends' horses or short trail rides on hired ones, my sister's horse experience in recent years scored near zero. No way my father wanted a spirited horse for his young daredevil daughter.

With introductions concluded, only one problem remained. As a quarter horse in the prime of his life, Frisky stood tall and straight, a good hike for my five-foot-two sister to reach his back. Add a blanket and Western saddle to his height, and she needed a stepladder or hefty boost to insert her foot in the stirrup, grab the saddle horn, and pull herself into the seat. Dismounting would be equivalent to jumping off the high diving board at a swimming pool.

This time my father smiled, and upon reflection I believe he chose Frisky for more than his docile disposition. The horse's height required my father to be with my sister every time she rode Frisky. Oh, she might sneak the short distance down the road from our house to where he was boarded on a friend's farm. But no way she carried the saddle, bridle, and blanket that far by herself. Although my sister was well known for finding creative solutions to accomplish her goals, Frisky's height prevented her from piling the gear in our little red wagon, pulling it to the farm, and enjoying a solo ride. "Have father, will gallop" was the only way.

On their first ride together, my father showed my sister how to place the blanket on Frisky's back, ease the saddle into place, and adjust the belly bands. Some folks might use the terms cinch strap and rear billet, but in our southern location we called them belly bands. My father never failed to amuse us with his alternative names or pronunciation of words, some of which we continue to use as family jokes.

Once Sarge situated herself in the saddle and my father double-checked the straps and bridle, the three of them walked along the fence row for a good ways. With a black mane and tail, Frisky sported a smattering of white above his front hooves and carried himself well, following behind my father and appearing to know he transported precious cargo on his back. As my sister mastered using her knees in coordination with the reins to guide Frisky, my father let them meander alone in the field with strict instructions not to gallop. For one of the few times I observed, she obeyed him. Wow, Frisky had no idea he made equestrian history that day as the horse who trained my sister to listen and learn.

Each time she rode Frisky, my father allowed them to do more together. My sister recalls many gallops on sunny afternoons and slow walks through the woods on the other side of the open fields. On every trip, my father took her to the farm, watched her ride, and helped her care for Frisky. Were all the rides error free? Nope, a few mishaps occurred. One time Frisky stepped on my sister's foot by mistake. When she yelped, Frisky nuzzled her face as if to say, "Oops, I'm sorry."

Another incident involved the saddle. As always, my father re-checked every buckle and strap after hoisting Sarge into the saddle. After a pleasant and uneventful ride, Sarge headed Frisky back to where my father always waited on them. With flat ground in front of them all the way to the fence, Frisky picked up his speed enough for a steady gallop at a clip my sister encouraged. What happened next is up for debate. Sarge claims she was in the saddle one second and on the ground the next one, a little sore and bruised but with nothing broken.

After inspecting the saddle and Frisky, my father questioned her about how many times Frisky took a pit stop and the amount of fertilizer he deposited. If you spend time around horses, you know they deposit considerable amounts of the aromatic product everywhere they go. My father concluded Frisky's last pit stop lessened his girth just enough to cause saddle slippage toward the left side. Yep, adequate tension on those belly bands is important for keeping the saddle in place and the rider in the saddle. But Frisky's reaction touched us all. After realizing he was rider-free, that affectionate horse stopped, circled back, and checked on his best buddy.

A good number of years have elapsed since my sister and Frisky rode those fields and enjoyed each other's company. During that time, we grew up, went to college, and married the men of our dreams. Children and grandchildren arrived, and after long lives our parents passed away. One day recently while sitting on a warm southern beach and watching the tide roll in, Sarge and I remi-nisced about our childhood and all the extraordinary times we shared as a family. Over the years we played hard, laughed loud, cried during many tender moments, and ate an abundance of de-licious homecooked Southern food. We wouldn't trade any of those precious times and our memories of them for all the money in the world.

During one of our beach conversations, my sister and I talked about Frisky. As expected, her memories of him were clearer than mine, and she fondly recounted his sweet and gentle ways. Later when I gave more thought to what she said and the time period when Frisky became part of our lives, I may have discovered why my parents bought him for her. Yes, I still remember my initial shock, but perhaps my younger sister experienced equal surprise at how much our lives had changed in those eight months before we got Frisky.

The September before we attended the Kentucky Derby, I entered high school. Within weeks, my focus shifted from activities I once did with Sarge to ones she couldn't attend. In previous school years, my mother always included her in my class events because we attended the same school and had many of the same friends. Not anymore. At my new school, I immersed myself in friends, sports, and clubs my sister didn't know or understand. Instead of two sisters doing everything together, we spent more and more time apart. Did I recognize the change or its impact? Nope. Like most teenagers, my world rotated around me, myself, and I.

To my parents' credit, I believe they saw my sister's need for a new friend and took appropriate action. When Sarge expressed interest in a horse of her own, they responded by acquiring Frisky. All four of us faced a new chapter in our lives and adapted to the necessary adjustments. While one parent shuttled and chaperoned me and my new friends to high school activities, the other one spent quality time with Sarge and her horse.

My mother delighted in being part of my high school fun. As a teenager growing up during the Great Depression and World War II, she worked after classes and participated in few school events. For my father's part, I'm guessing he realized I needed the guidance of my mother as I developed into a young woman. I also suspect he relished the adventure and excitement of his younger daughter having a horse of her own. In only a few years, Sarge would be in high school and no longer his little girl. He wasn't going to miss being a kid again with her and sharing those golden moments together.

My sister's childhood quarter horse gave each person in our family an incredible gift—the specific opportunity we needed at a significant time in our lives. To my parents, Frisky offered a second chance to experience what they missed at our age. To my sister, he rescued her from loneliness and filled her empty afternoons and weekends with joy and accomplishment. To me, that brown horse with the black mane and tail represents two different gifts separated by a span of years.

Although I didn't comprehend Frisky's importance while I attended high school, his presence back then furnished me the freedom to mature and cultivate new interests. Nowadays, I appreciate how the memory of him made me realize my sister and I have completed a circle in our relationship. Once again, we take every possible occasion to be together and share this journey we call life, enjoying it through a forever bond of love.

Have the two of us changed over the years? Yes and no. Neither one of us has ridden a horse in ages. I'm still taller than she is, and she's dialed down her mischief a little.

Is she still a tad bossy? Our cousin called her Sarge the other day. What do you think?

5

Walk On

Kim Peterson

Hard times come to us all—people and animals alike. Even daily life requires courage to walk the journey before us. The courage to keep going.

One of the most courageous creatures I've ever known was a beautiful horse called Nibbles. I first met the mare in 2000 at LoveWay Therapeutic Equestrian Services in Middlebury, Indiana. LoveWay, founded in 1973, compassionately works to transform lives through therapeutic equestrian experiences. Nibbles was one of about twenty horses and ponies providing therapy and interaction for people ages three to sixty-five with special needs.

My husband recently joined the numerous volunteers in our community who gave their time to help. Although Sean wasn't part of the human team assisting students, he wanted me to join him to meet LoveWay's equine team and to see them in action. So we drove to the bucolic setting and turned into the long dirt driveway that climbed between two pastures to a parking area in front of a sprawling building. This barn housed the offices, stable, and indoor arena.

There, I first encountered the horses and ponies. Some hung their heads over their stall doors, accepting a pat on the nose or the scratching of an ear. Others, patiently cross tied in the barn aisle, were being groomed by students guided by volunteers. In the arena, more horses participated in a small class, giving their riders a workout.

All the horses with riders were amazing. But one truly stood out. A white mare walked holding her head at an angle, a child on her back, following her leader and listening for any commands about what to do next.

I asked Sean, "Why is she cocking her head like that?"

"Nibbles is blind in one eye."

As I continued to observe, I realized this horse was keeping the lead volunteer in her sights, watching for nonverbal cues, while one ear was pointed back listening to what happened behind her. She was impressive and steady.

Horses accept you how you are, whether you have autism, multiple sclerosis, cerebral palsy, Down syndrome, traumatic brain injury, or any other diagnoses. Therapy horses don't worry about the label. Undeterred by wheelchairs and crutches, unafraid of weak or misshapen limbs, careful with people who couldn't communicate clearly, Nibbles provided mobility for those who may not otherwise have had opportunity.

Nibbles's steady responses provided her young rider with important exercise. Basic horseback riding uses muscles important to walking. Participation can improve coordination, muscle tone, range of motion, and balance. A volunteer leads the horse when the student sits in the saddle. Other volunteers walk on either side of the rider to help with safety and stability, telling the horse when to "stop" or "stand" or "walk on."

When the child finished his session that day, the side walkers helped him dismount at a specially designed platform. The gentle mare welcomed his pats and nuzzled his hand.

Then Nibbles was led back to the stable area, where her tack was removed and she was groomed by other students and volunteers. Even just interacting with the horses often builds confidence. Nibbles's rapport with all the students was lovely and inspiring.

Several years passed as Sean continued his efforts at LoveWay. His role was to care for the equine team. He mucked stalls, fed and watered, administered medications, and did anything else the horses required. He smoothed the terrain near the barn when winter weather created deep ruts. He mended fences and gates. He repaired stalls that required attention. He helped keep the horses healthy and safe.

I heard about all his adventures and occasionally accompanied him when my heavy teaching schedule allowed. Some horses retired and new therapy horses came along, so I had to meet these equine miracle workers as well as greet my longtime horse acquaintances.

With sadness, I learned Nibbles had contracted an infection in her remaining eye. Treatment didn't solve the problem. Eventually, the eye had to be removed. I feared the worst, but she returned to LoveWay, where she was beloved by all—staff, students, and volunteers. Being with the people she knew, surrounded by the familiar sounds of her busy home, Nibbles recuperated.

I was surprised when she eventually resumed her previous duties. No wonder everyone flocked to this lovable mare who shared her courage with the students. The next time I watched Nibbles in action, though sightless, she was gentle with her rider, listened for all the cues, and—without hesitation—walked on.

When my schedule changed about a year later, I was exhausted from more than a decade of overworking and uncertain how to move into a less stressful job arrangement. I was grappling with intense anxiety in crowds and in new situations.

Sean thought time with the horses would be refreshing, and he asked me to join him as a LoveWay volunteer. Of course, I responded with enthusiasm. I wasn't much of a horsewoman, but I could muck a stall with the best. I also learned to portion out flakes of hay as well as mix food, add beet pulp, and stir in sweet feed according to the chart specifying each horse's diet.

Sean knew my hesitation around horses. Although I love them, I tend to be nervous, even a little afraid around the large animals. But on my first day as a volunteer, my husband showed me where the tack was stored, let me into the feed room, which smelled pretty tasty, and reintroduced me to the two friendly barn cats. He gave me instructions, and we soon cleaned all the stalls, measured the food, and filled the water buckets. He took care of preparing any medications. We even fed the barn cats and changed their water.

Time to bring in the horses. Sean walked me to the side pasture. When we reached the lush grassy area, we were surrounded, and my ever-present anxiety rose. Sean reacquainted me with Cosby, a kind pony about my height.

Though my heart was pounding, the pony stood her ground and remained unflappable among the pushy mares. Her nerve made this almost seem doable.

I asked about the path, and Sean assured me Cosby knew the way. "You'll be fine."

So, I mustered my courage and grasped the rope he had just snapped onto her halter. I took a step, and Cosby joined right in. I was to lead her to the barn, which was a bit of a misnomer. She led me. Every time I increased my pace to keep up, she sped up too.

When we arrived at the barn—I breathless and Cosby having glanced dubiously over her shoulder at me from time to time—the pony led me to her stall, where her full feed bucket awaited. After I removed the lead rope and latched her stall door, she didn't give me another glance. I'm pretty sure she wondered where they found this volunteer.

Once my breathing slowed, I patted one of the barn cats and told the pony I was heading out. The snuffling sound of Cosby's eating never paused.

My next assignment was to fetch Nibbles. I couldn't spot the mare anywhere. Sean said she was probably in the farthest pasture out by the tree line. After several minutes of instructions and reassuring discussion, I took the lead rope he gave me and started across the fields, hands trembling. As I moved slightly uphill, I saw that Sean was right. Nibbles, white coat shining against the dark green forest behind her, was way out there.

How did a blind horse wander so far? And how would I get her all the way back to the barn?

I needn't have felt nervous. Nibbles had heard us begin the evening ritual of moving the horses and ponies, bringing out hay, and more. By the time I drew near to the back pasture to collect her, she already had begun her slow walk toward the gate that led into the next pasture. A horse always knows when it's suppertime!

As she ambled my way, I spoke to her across the field. Her head turned briefly. Then she focused on the gate again, which surprised me. But as we both neared the opening from different directions, I realized the barn staff had hung wind chimes that rang in the soft breeze. Nibbles was following their delicate tinkling, adjusting her pace and angle until she reached the open gate, then walked through into the lower pasture where I met her.

She greeted me with a soft whicker, her mane shifting with the wind.

A little hesitant, I approached her while talking. I patted her neck, enjoying the smoothness of her coat.

I told her how smart she was, snapped the lead rope to her halter, and said, "Walk on."

Together, we headed for the barn. I placed a hand on her shoulder, and she leaned into my hand. Tears came as I felt her courage to trust someone she barely knew to lead her safely to her stall.

I jabbered nervously on that first stroll, but Nibbles kept pace with me, swishing her tail as we moved in a sweeping arc around the hay barn and downhill, then back to the left toward the stable.

I spent the next year and a half outpaced by Cosby and walking beside Nibbles. Both were kind, aware of my fears. Accepting my limitations, they showed me compassion and affection.

Nibbles, though, inspired me. She gave me courage. Courage to do what I hadn't been able to do before.

Nibbles was an older mare when I met her. After she retired from transforming students' lives in the arena, Nibbles remained at LoveWay, loved and cared for. Even though she is gone now, I often think of her and her intrepid determination to keep going no matter what.

I regularly pray for that kind of courage. I pray that I—like that sweet white mare—can face each day and walk on.

6

Tiny Tim

Peggy Frezon

I waded through the tall grass, careful not to scuff my shiny new imitation-leather cowboy boots with the fancy gold embroidery. The boots I'd seen on the department store shelf but never imagined I would get to own. And, although I could barely believe it, there I was in my brand-new boots, about to realize the dream I'd had for practically all my nine years.

Like many girls my age, I was horse-obsessed. My bedroom walls were covered with posters of majestic horses with flowing manes. I read *Black Beauty* and *Misty of Chincoteague*. I trotted well-loved horse figurines around makeshift cardboard corrals. But the closest I'd ever been to a real horse was a pony at the county fair petting zoo. That was, until a few weeks earlier when my mom gave me a certificate for honest-to-goodness, actual horseback riding lessons for my birthday.

"Really and truly?" I'd asked as I threw my arms around her. I felt as if I were floating high, high up with the pretty pink party balloons. Never before had I received such an amazing gift. But my parents were going through a divorce, and Mom must have wanted to give me something special. I knew that she sensed how anxious I'd been feeling, how I'd been spending hours alone in my room, worrying about how our lives would change.

She tried to talk to me. "It seems scary now. But everything will be fine. You just have to trust." How could I trust what I didn't know? I believed in God. But how was he going to help a matter like this? My dad had already moved out. Soon we were going to move too. Everything would be different.

But now, making my way up to a small, fenced ring in the middle of open pasture, I could forget about all that for a while. I was finally going to get up close to a horse, to experience the thrill of riding horseback! I wiggled my toes in my new boots. They felt stiff and strange.

I joined the other boys and girls gathered by the gate. Several horses of every size and color were tied up to the fence. A young man in jeans took the reins of the most enormous white horse I'd ever seen. I took a step back. While I loved horses from a distance, up close they were a lot more intimidating than I'd imagined. Those long, hooved legs. The brawny flanks. All together it was the most beautiful, and most frightening, animal I'd ever been near.

The instructor presented the horse to a boy, who eagerly scrambled up the wooden mounting block and into the saddle. One by one the instructors matched the horses with eager riders. My knees shook. I shied to the back of the group until I was the last one left. By now I was scared silly, staring at the ground, my stomach twisting in knots.

One of the instructors took my hand and smiled. "I think I have just the horse for you." She untied the reins of a jet-black horse with a shaggy black mane and big, soft eyes. "This is Tiny Tim," she said.

I nodded. He was smaller, for sure, than any of the other horses. I inched closer to him and hesitantly put my hand on his neck. Could I trust him? He bobbed his head and snorted. I laughed and followed him into the riding ring. Tiny Tim stood perfectly still as the instructor taught me how to put my foot in the stirrup and swing my other leg over. Tiny Tim shifted as I landed in the saddle, as if he was getting a sense of me on his back, figuring out how we fit together. I stroked his mane. "I'll be your friend," I said.

The woman instructor told us to place our feet firmly in the stirrups. I slid my dusty cowboy boots where they belonged. "Keep the reins slightly loose," she said. "Now give your horse a gentle squeeze with your legs."

I wanted to go, but not very fast, so I didn't push hard. Tiny Tim didn't move. I tried again, a little harder. He stepped sideways. "It's okay," I said softly, and to my surprise he moved forward. He followed the other horses around the circle. With each lap I sat taller, no longer afraid of being so high up. Things may have been a mess in real life, but at that moment everything was perfect. Here this huge (to me!) animal allowed me on his back, and we were comfortably moving together. He must have trusted me. And I finally felt that I could trust Tiny Tim too.

I looked out at the grassy fields ahead. They were beautiful. It was the most calm and happy I'd felt in months. That is, until the horse ahead of me, the big white horse, alarmingly reared up. In one swift motion it jumped over the fence. The boy atop clung to the horn of the saddle. I caught my breath. Every muscle in my body wanted to get down and run away, but I didn't even know how to dismount.

In an instant, an instructor had things under control and returned the horse and boy, unharmed, to the arena. If she explained what had happened to cause such behavior, I didn't know. I was solely focused on getting out of there. I didn't enjoy the rest of my lesson. Instead, I prayed I'd get through it alive, until at last I was allowed to climb off.

The next week I didn't want to return. "I don't feel well," I said, which was true. I was a mess. I could barely breathe. What if the same thing happened to me?

"Just try," my mother urged. Well, maybe she could get me there, but she couldn't force me up on a horse. The very thing I'd dreamed of for years was nothing I wanted anymore. I pulled on my cowboy boots and sulked to the car.

The other kids gathered by the fence for the lesson didn't seem worried at all. Even the boy himself looked eager. The instructors helped everyone onto their horses. I wasn't going to get on. Not me. Too scary. The horses were led into the riding arena. All but Tiny Tim. He stood, all alone, waiting for me. He lowered his head and munched some grass. I felt sorry for him. He hadn't done anything wrong. He hadn't been anxious or nervous like me. He hadn't followed when the horse in front of him bolted. Maybe I could give him another chance.

I walked over slowly and touched his neck. He didn't move away. "What do you think, Tim?" I asked. "Should we try again?" I looked into his eyes, eyes that seemed to say, "Trust me." He stood very still, as if he knew even the slightest move might send me running.

"Ready?" the instructor asked. She led Tiny Tim into the ring with the others and reminded me how to get up into the saddle. I stepped on the block, pushed my cowboy boot into the stirrup. After mounting, I swallowed hard and squeezed my legs. Tiny Tim stepped slowly and carefully. That feeling, that special feeling, of riding a horse began to come back to me. "We're doing it," I said. And as I rode, I thought, if I could do this, maybe I could also do something as difficult as navigating life after my parents' divorce.

There were many reasons I wanted to take riding lessons that year. But I never knew that among them was to have the opportunity to prove that I was brave, that I could do something difficult and frightening. Who'd have thought that a tiny black horse would give me that chance?

And best of all, Tiny Tim and I became friends. At the next lesson I brought him an apple, and he nuzzled my arm. We learned to trot. It would be my only formal experience riding horses, but it came at a time when I so desperately needed a friend to show me that something scary could turn out well. Now, whenever I need a reminder of that, I think of Tiny Tim, and I know that fears and uncertainties can gallop away on the shiny black hooves of the smallest little horse in the riding ring.

7

Felix the Zebra

Tahlia Fischer

If you had told me when I was a kid growing up in California that I would one day become a rescuer of horses, I would have been very excited. Because from the time I was a child, it seemed like animals came to me. In turn, I always found solace in them.

My parents, both my sisters, and I loved animals. We especially liked dogs—puppies and dogs were my first friends. In our home, we had Rottweilers from Germany, Tosas from Japan when they were first imported to the United States, and mastiffs from France. We all loved horses too, but we didn't have them or any other large animals. Owning horses seemed more like a hobby for the very successful.

Nevertheless, I fell in love with horses at the age of three. I vividly recall being placed way up on the back of a horse behind my cousin. I hung on to my cousin for dear life, and I was thrilled to be there. The horse started bucking because of a horsefly, and I was still excited. My love of horses was born then and lived quietly inside me. Like many girls at the time, I fed that desire by collecting Breyer horse statues.

I grew up and went to college. The degree I received wasn't really getting me work, so I waited tables. It was while I was a waitress twelve years ago that my love for horses moved out of my imagination and into my life and took over.

I was driving to church one Sunday morning and stopped for a red light. Off to my side was a junkyard, and on this day, I noticed three horses standing in it. All three were emaciated. I had not seen them before, and it troubled me. But the light changed, and I drove on to church.

The sermon that day had to do with stepping up and taking action when nobody else will. It made me think of the horses I'd just seen. I took the sermon as a sign to do something, so after church, I drove to the junkyard. There was an emergency number written on a private property sign. I called, which put me in touch with the owner of the junkyard.

I asked about the horses, which he claimed were not his. I asked him if the owner might be willing to sell the horses. He said yes, all three could go for $3,000. Reluctantly, I told him that was too much for me. I also reminded him what poor shape the horses were in. We made no deal that day, but the next day he called me back. He asked me what I would be willing to pay. I told him $300 for all three. He agreed to it.

Now I found myself the owner of three, not-in-good-shape horses. My first problem was that I had no place to put horses. Oh, and I had no experience with horses, either! I was a single woman waiting tables in the expensive state of California. What was I thinking?

I managed to find someone to transport the horses to a friend's house a half hour away where they could stay for a while. Another friend gave me a thousand dollars to pay for the vet, and we got the horses healthy. Then a lady in Tehachapi, not too far away from where I lived, offered me the use of her field. This was a generous offer. We moved my three horses to their new home and watched them thrive.

Sometime later, my sister learned on social media that there was a donkey in trouble in Texas. She encouraged me to save this donkey, and I managed to do it. I was so excited that when I met that sweet donkey—all the way from Texas—I started crying. I hoped he knew that he would be okay now.

Much to my surprise, my grandfather surprised me by telling me how much he loved donkeys. *Grandpa loves donkeys?* I had no idea. It turned out he worked with donkeys during WWII in France and Germany. Corps of equines helped the war efforts on both sides, and Grandpa told us stories I'd never heard before about his wartime experiences involving these sturdy animals. He got involved in the care of this donkey, and we had good family time bonding over that.

By now, I had a job working full-time in sales. But my sister decided that I should start an official animal rescue. She reminded me that I'd been saving animals since childhood. She also reminded me what I had written on Facebook—that my passion was animals and that my hope was to someday help them and, in the process, help humans too.

She helped me figure it out. I filed for and received nonprofit status. Then we rescued a Thoroughbred, a mini horse, and an unhandled quarter horse and her filly. Then a few more animals came in from Northern California. I was still keeping them in my friend's backyard—about three acres that he let us use. Eventually we acquired more acreage across from a pistachio orchard and put down roots for an actual rescue. We named it "All Seated in a Barn."

As you can imagine, the rescue became my whole life. At first, I was the one cleaning the stalls, building social media, and paying for things by draining my savings account. Fundraising was difficult, and I had to get creative. I started having events so people could come meet the animals, and that helped with feed. I posted on Instagram and got lots of followers. Just before COVID hit, we had about fifty animals and some volunteers. My boss told me I couldn't keep working like this, and I'd need to choose my job or my rescue. I chose the rescue. Then COVID hit, and I realized I would have been laid off anyway.

During COVID, I was dating someone long distance in Texas. One time when I visited, he asked if I'd ever been to a livestock auction. I had not, and it seemed like a good idea to go. Maybe I could save a horse or two. I posted a video on social media that I was going to my first auction, and my video went viral. Even a celebrity shared it, and, unbelievably, I received $40,000 to help me rescue animals at this auction. I bought and rescued ninety-two horses and donkeys.

The next morning, I woke up thinking once again, *What have I done?*

As it turned out, just before the auction I had run into a friend of mine I hadn't seen in years, and it came up in conversation that he had three acres of land. I got in touch with him and said, "I have ninety-two animals and no place to put them. I need your land." He came through, and we boarded them for as long as it took to find other rescues or homes for the animals.

I went to another auction and acquired eighty more animals. We were erecting pens and turnouts everywhere. Again, other rescues and sanctuaries stepped up and took the animals. People told me I was crazy rescuing so many animals. But I always believed that this was what I was supposed to be doing and that things would all work out. And they would. In the meantime, the operation continued to grow.

Which leads me to Felix.

A few years ago, a friend told me about a three-month-old baby zebra for sale online. In the United States, it's legal to hunt zebras on private game ranches in several states. People pay to do it. The ranchers sell the zebra foal as a bottle baby and report that the mother died; in fact, the mother was hunted. The rancher gets paid for the hunted zebra and is also paid when someone takes the baby. This ranch was charging quite a bit for the baby, and I knew I couldn't afford it, so the friend offered to buy the foal and have subsequent donations pay him back.

A couple guys from my barn drove to Wisconsin to pick up the colt. When he was unloaded back home, I was smitten. This baby was the first zebra foal I'd ever seen. He was about the size of a Great Dane, and he was very shy with beautiful eyes. It felt surreal to see this little guy. My heart melted. But my brain was saying, *I hope I didn't make a mistake taking this on.* I wanted to do right by this colt, but I had some fear of the unknown. Zebras truly are wild animals, and I'd heard stories of them turning on humans. I didn't want anyone getting hurt as he got older.

But I made the commitment and named him. I looked at him and thought, *He looks like a Felix.* Maybe all that strong black-and-white striping reminded me of the black-and-white cartoon *Felix the Cat.* Whatever the reason, the name stuck, and he has been Felix ever since.

We had a miniature baby donkey, so we put the baby zebra with him. Felix arrived with a pair of jeans that had been worn by his previous owner. For three days, I wore those jeans. After three days I hung up my own jeans with his previous owner's jeans on the fence post near Felix. I eventually took the man's jeans away and left mine. This helped, but it still took a good three months for Felix to see me as okay and start coming around.

Eventually we moved Felix in with an old, wise, sweet gelding who was more comfortable with people. So began Felix's socialization with humans, and it worked, though he bonded with me faster than with others. He also preferred women over men. As he got older, he trusted me enough that I could halter-train him.

A zebra is an equine, but I learned that my zebra did not really act like a horse. To me, Felix seemed more like a cat—aloof and solitary—plus, like a cat, he expressed a lot with his tail. When he was done with his human or another animal, he was done, and his tail let us know before he kicked. The horses were terrified of him. He didn't whinny, he didn't bray, and at feeding time, he had his own sound: *a-hoyt, a-hoyt, a-hoyt.*

In many ways, he acted like a little prince. But let me be clear—it's difficult to own a zebra. In the wild, zebras innately run from lions. Kicking is their first line of defense, and they use it freely. Their hind end is their weapon. Horses kick straight back—but zebras can also kick sideways. Obviously, this was going to be a challenge. The farrier said I'd have to figure this out myself.

So I spent special time with Felix, touching his back end and lifting his hooves so I could clean his feet. It worked. He's now two years old and the size of a small pony, and I can trim his feet with the farrier. I can take him on walks, but he does not get ridden. We use him to educate people—that they should *not* own zebras as pets.

I love Felix. This is his home, and he has many animal and human friends. Felix reminds me how grateful I am that I've been able to make equine rescue my passion. It's not easy. It can break your heart. Sometimes I need to make decisions I don't want to make.

But the rewards are so great. And I know this work is my personal mission, the reason I'm here. I wouldn't change my situation for anything.

8

Bolt the Colt and the Gramma Mare

Kristi Ross

Last night's rain clouds gave way to a glorious day. As I drove down my tree-lined driveway and admired the brilliant blue sky and the white cotton candy clouds, I was excited. I couldn't wait to tell the ladies of my church prayer group the news. It was because of them I was feeling so thankful today. They were the ones who had prayed so hard for poor little Bolt.

The two-month-old colt had been an orphan for three days. The first time I offered him a bottle of milk replacer, he refused. The next time I brought a bottle of milk up to his lips and tried to get the nipple into his mouth, he threw his head away. I grabbed him again and tried to get him to suck my milk-soaked finger. This time, he nearly bit me. Once more, I stuck the bottle into the side of his mouth, but he bit the end of the nipple off. Milk sprayed all over the both of us. I could do nothing to get him to suck.

Weaning is one of the most stressful events of a foal's life, and two-month-old Bolt's weaning came way too early. He would not take the bottles of milk replacer. I thought about using a feeding tube. I could use it to squirt milk down Bolt's throat, but there was no way

I could hold him still enough, and the danger of getting milk into his lungs was too great. Everyone who could help me lived too far away.

Then there was Rosie, my thirty-one-year-old gramma mare who was past the usual lifespan of a horse. In human years, she was over ninety years old. She had earned the right to live out her days on our ranch because of the amazing horses she had given us and how she bonded with all the babies. She was the perfect gramma, but she was so stressed about little Bolt not eating that she also refused to eat.

I tried coaxing her with fresh grain. She wouldn't even look at it. Usually, she was the first one to the feed pan. I added alfalfa to her regular grass hay, something she usually loved. Still, she wouldn't look at it. I added molasses to the grain, so that it smelled really good. Nothing. I kept changing out fresh hay and grain. I tried every trick I could think of, but neither Rosie nor Bolt would come near the feed.

On the third day, I watched Rosie and Bolt for several minutes before I walked toward the foal. Normally, he would trot up and turn his butt to me for a scratch. But today he barely looked at me, so I went to him. Rosie came near us. I reached out and put a hand on each horse and looked up to the sky. "Dear God, I need your help. Please show me what I need to do to get these horses to eat."

That afternoon I got my prayer ladies involved. I told them about little Bolt, and every one of them became invested in his welfare. When I told them about Rosie, they included her in their prayers. They frequently texted me, asking how Bolt and Rosie were doing. It was uplifting to have such support, but for a couple of days I saw little improvement.

Debby from the group texted that she didn't know much about horses other than when she walked out into her pasture and the neighbor's horses would come over to say hi. "Something completely settles over you when they look at you," Debbie said. "They look right into you. You can never deny that they feel deeply. I'm glad you're there for them." Each woman told me they were praying for Bolt and Rosie, but I don't believe any of us expected the amazing thing that was about to happen.

The following morning, I discovered the horses had moved. I could see Rosie's head above the hay feeder. *Is she eating?* I ran toward Rosie. As I came near, I couldn't believe what my eyes were seeing. Rosie had indeed eaten almost all her feed, but even more amazing, it looked for all the world as if Bolt was nursing.

I dropped to my hands and knees for a closer look. Bolt's little pink tongue grabbed the teat and began to suck. It was the sweetest thing ever.

At first, I thought it must not be more than a pacifier. Surely Rosie was too old and barren to produce real milk. But soon, I heard the slurp of sucking and saw real milk drip from Bolt's mouth. I burst into laughter, which startled little Bolt. He looked at me as if to say, "What's the problem?" Then he went right back to nursing.

I rose to my feet and stroked Rosie's neck. She simply stood there with her eyes closed. She was no longer eating; she was savoring the moment. I could see the emotion on her face and feel it emanating from her. It was pure love.

The next day I headed to my prayer group to relay the good news. As I turned into the parking lot, I thought about what a difference one week can make. Last week I was enveloped by sadness. This week I felt like a four-year-old on Christmas morning waiting for their parents to wake up.

"You won't believe it," I told the ladies. "Old Rosie is little Bolt's nurse mare!"

"But isn't that very unusual for an old horse to be able to nurse like that?" Sarah, one of the ladies, asked.

"Yes ma'am, it is. I thought it was impossible, so I called my vet. He said it happens, but it's rare."

The ladies were thrilled and oohed and ahhed over the pictures I showed them. We certainly called that an answer to prayer.

Today, two months later, Rosie and Bolt are thriving. Bolt got a new momma, and Rosie got to be a momma again. I was reminded that God really does love all his creatures.

9

A Star Is Born

Jan Epp

I grew up on a large farm in Wisconsin. We raised Guernsey milk cows, Angus beef cattle, sheep, pigs, horses, and Hackney ponies. I always wanted a donkey too. I had fallen in love with their sweet ways. But my dad said, "They are crazy and wild." So I didn't have one.

After I was married, my husband, Tom, and I moved to Michigan. We lived in the city for a time while we searched for a house in the country. Eventually we found a beautiful place on two and a half acres, and we moved in. Although my husband had lived in the city all his life, he adjusted very quickly to country life. In fact, he loved it. When thirty-six acres became available across the street from our house, we bought it.

My husband had always been a very buttoned-down kind of dresser. He practically wore a suit and tie to bed. Now that he had a farm, I encouraged him to buy a couple pairs of blue jeans. Instead, he bought several pairs. Once he started wearing jeans, I couldn't get him to wear a suit and tie again. I guess that I should have been more careful of what I wished for!

Of course, you can't live in the country without animals. After some discussion, Tom and I headed to a sheep auction in the next county just to "observe." Of course, we brought home sheep—fifteen bred, registered Suffolk ewes. At first, we housed them in our extra garage, but an unhappy neighbor reported us to the township. We immediately built a barn on the thirty-six acres.

All was well. Then we began hearing the yipping of coyotes at night, and although they never showed themselves, we became concerned for our sheep and their lambs. We understood that donkeys would make excellent guard animals—they're hardwired to repel canines—and we decided we needed a couple. Finally, I was getting my donkey!

The Bureau of Land Management sells the mustangs and burros that they round up, so we went to their website and completed an application to adopt two burros. It took several weeks to get an answer back, but then we were notified that we were approved. They had an adoption event coming up at the fairgrounds in Janesville, Wisconsin. We lived five hours from Janesville, and the event was starting at 8:00 a.m. Since adoptions were on a first-come-first-served basis, we needed to leave home at 3:00 a.m. so we could be one of the first in line to adopt two burros.

Tom and I got our two boys, Travis and Augie, up at 2:00 a.m. and headed outside to get the trailer hitched to the truck. Our two beautiful gray rescue cats, Suzy and Lucy, came from the barn to hang out with us. We petted them, hitched everything up, and headed out for Janesville by 2:30 a.m. The boys fell asleep in the bac seat of the truck.

We arrived at Janesville at 7:30 a.m. There were six trailers ahead of us. So much for being the first in line. We parked the trailer so we could go view the burros. When we got out of the truck, we heard a cat meowing. We opened the trailer, and there was Lucy. She apparently had crawled into the trailer back home. In the dark we didn't see her. The boys caught her and put her in the truck. She would later have a great ride home with the boys petting her the whole way.

The adoption process began. Everyone was taking a couple of burros, and we had concerns there might not be any available when our time came. Every adopter was given a half hour to pick their burros, and we waited several hours for our number to come up.

By then, only two donkeys remained. The jack was dark brown, and he was perfect except for a large piece of his left ear missing from a fight with another burro. He was still a nice-looking jack. We adopted him and named him Jethro after the character on *The Beverly Hillbillies*. Ellie May, also named for the TV show, was a pinkish-looking jenny and so beautiful. We were pleased to acquire such good-looking burros.

We loaded up and happily returned home with our new burros (and our adventurous cat). Once we started the taming process, it didn't take long before Jethro and Ellie May were eating ginger snaps from our hands. They had wonderful personalities. Best of all, they were excellent guard burros for our sheep. Wherever the sheep were, Jethro and Ellie May were nearby. They chased out coyotes and even any strange dogs who came into the pasture. Once they arrived, we didn't lose any of our ewes or lambs to coyotes.

We eventually realized that Ellie May was pregnant. We had no idea when we'd see a baby, but it happened on Christmas Day. When we went to the barn to do chores, there was a beautiful brown baby jack. We were excited to have a baby burro, and his parents were so proud of him. Since he was born on Christmas, we named him Jesus. He was a very lovable animal who learned from his parents how to be a guard burro.

A couple years after Jesus was born, our oldest son, Augie, attended Michigan State College of Veterinary Medicine. He had a friend there who grew up on a large sheep ranch not far away. His family was losing sometimes ten lambs a night to coyotes. Augie offered Jesus to his friend's family to guard their sheep, and he delivered the burro the next day. The family immediately put him in the pasture with their ewes and lambs. Once Jesus was with their sheep, the family never lost another lamb to coyotes.

Jesus's picture wound up on the cover of the magazine *Michigan Shepherd*, and an article inside praised him for saving all those lambs. Of course, we were so proud of him. Today Jesus is still on the ranch, successfully doing what comes naturally to him—protecting sheep and lambs from coyotes.

I'm doing what comes naturally to me too—bringing home donkeys, miniature donkeys, and mules, many of them rescues. They love their ginger snaps. And they are just as sweet as my childhood self always knew they would be.

YOU SAY BURRO, I SAY BURRITO . . .

Burro is the Spanish term for donkey, and English-speaking handlers use either word. Burro comes from a Latin term for small horse. The word also made its way into cuisine—that stuffed, round look of a tasty burrito is a nod to the sturdy pack burro.

The Year Dad Got It Right

Claudia Wolfe St. Clair

When my parents were alive, I could count on a clandestine phone call from my dad sometime around Thanksgiving.

"What does your mother want for Christmas?"

After *decades* together, Dad remained clueless.

"A chain saw. She wants a chain saw."

Long pause. "You're kiddin' me."

"Dad. She wants a chain saw."

The ensuing conversation went all over the place. *Why* does she want a chain saw? It's dangerous. She'll injure herself.

You get the idea. He just could not wrap his head around a request so far out of left field.

Actually, her desire for a chain saw was entirely practical. Their home on Lake Erie endured massive spring storms. Those storms deposited whole tree trunks and other large things that required a chain saw to reduce the debris field to manageable levels. Most of their firewood came from these spring storms. Mom planned on using it herself because Mom was fearless.

There was one Thanksgiving that came and went without the annual "What does your mother want for Christmas?" call. The year was 1973. All on his own, Dad got it absolutely right!

63

It would have been difficult to miss what occupied my mother's attention that year. Mom was *completely* obsessed with Triple Crown winner Secretariat. She had watched him win the Kentucky Derby. She counted the days until the Preakness. Another win. By the time the Belmont Stakes rolled around, she could barely contain herself. Secretariat won the Belmont by thirty-one lengths in two minutes and twenty-four seconds. At the time, it was a new world record.

Secretariat was the media darling. Mom started collecting news clippings and magazine articles. She bought memorabilia honoring Secretariat. Before long, she set up a shrine to Secretariat on her desk that upstaged photos of my brother and me. He and I could not compete with the Triple Crown winner.

Mom and I spoke on the phone often. Those were the days when the length of long-distance calls was reflected on the phone bill. She and I were *always* in trouble over the length of our conversations. That year the calls were pretty one-sided. Mom talked *endlessly* about Secretariat. Dad noticed.

Dad decided to surprise Mom with a trip to Paris, Kentucky, for Christmas. Destination? Claiborne Farm, home of Secretariat. He had her pack for a few days and told her nothing. Southward bound on I-75. It's a five-hour drive from Toledo, Ohio, to Paris, Kentucky.

Apparently when Dad made the turn for Paris, Mom squealed! She knew Secretariat was stabled there. She knew *everything* there was to know about Secretariat.

Once checked in, she couldn't wait to leave the hotel and get to the farm. Mom was overjoyed as they passed through the imposing gates. Even in winter, there were beautiful rolling hills and a tree-lined drive to the parking area. It was a long walk to the stable that housed Secretariat.

There he was in the paddock above the stable! Without hesitation, Mom marched right up to the fence. Never one to miss any adulation, Secretariat put his head over the fence and down within her reach. Making eye to eye contact, Mom gave him loving strokes on his muzzle, which he received quietly. It was a perfect moment for Mom—a dream come true and the thrill of a lifetime. All thanks to Dad.

In their fifty-four years together, this was their best Christmas. Dad, who could be pretty obtuse, gave Mom the one thing she wanted most without asking me. And Mom? She was filled with awe and gratitude that Dad gave her an experience she would treasure as long as she lived. It was incredibly special that they shared this moment. Dad was very pleased with himself.

This wonderful Christmas gift-giving, however, was an anomaly in their marriage. From 1974 onward, Dad resumed his annual "What does your mother what for Christmas?" calls.

So you might be wondering . . . did he get her the chain saw she wanted? He did. But I think he slept with one eye open the rest of his life.

11

The Black Pony

Chris Kent

The horizon in the east was just beginning to blush a faint crimson. Ghost-like mist rose over the cool river as it flowed between towering ebony spruce. The ridge beyond the bend in the river glowed as if tipped with gold leaf.

I watched this splendor unfold through the kitchen window as I warmed my hands around a morning cup of coffee. A mile from the nearest road, our log home was nestled at the end of a narrow gravel driveway. Rarely did a visitor say, "I was just passing by and thought I'd stop in." Thus, you can imagine my surprise on that early morning when the door burst open and my cousin Lori, without even a hello, shouted, "Don't you have enough to do? Now you have a pony?"

"A pony? I don't have a pony." I turned toward the door, setting my coffee cup on the kitchen island.

"There's one standing out by the barn." Lori's hands rested on her hips and her feet were planted firmly in the hallway. "It's black. Just a little one. Right by the barn. Just standing there."

"Oh no, that's the apple press covered with a black tarp. I didn't get it put away yesterday after we finished making juice." My husband had recently suffered a severe back injury, so work was piling up and jobs were not getting done as quickly as usual. "I was going to take care of it when I let the horses out."

"That's no apple press. I'm telling you, it's a pony," Lori insisted. "Come on, I'll show you."

Realizing any attempt to convince her differently would be to no avail, I slipped on my rubber boots and reached for my barn jacket on the hook near the door. "Okay, let's go take a look at this mystery pony you're seeing."

Early light cast long shadows across the yard as we walked toward the barn. A big snowshoe hare hopped from a hiding spot under a spruce tree, his fur already mottled, his oversized feet fringed with ashen hair. Soon he would be completely white, his winter camouflage, only the tips of his ears retaining the summer brown. Our two horses nickered from their stalls, a usual morning greeting as they heard my feet crunching in the gravel. All part of their morning ritual of conversation, three treats, and outside for the day.

As I turned the corner in front of the building, there it was, a Shetland pony standing quietly outside the barn, nose pressed against the door. I spoke softly as we approached, concerned I might startle him. I cautiously touched a shoulder, checked the gender, rubbed his neck, and scratched his ears. The pony exhibited no fear. He seemed extremely comfortable in arriving, unannounced, at this location. He turned his head toward me for a moment, then immediately resumed focus on the barn, ears forward, listening. He wore a green halter, his feet were trimmed, and he had no visible injuries. From all appearances he seemed healthy.

Knowing Shetland ponies can be a little feisty, I was cautious as I took ahold of the halter. He did not move and seemed to have no intent to leave. "Well, Black Pony, where did you come from?" I had already mentally inventoried the neighborhood, as distant as it was. There were no ponies in the area, and in fact, no other horses. There were thousands of acres of national forest, miles of river, swamps, sloughs, and few roads. The nearest farm was miles away.

"I told you so, it's a pony," Lori stated emphatically, pointing her finger.

I shrugged my shoulders. "Well, you were right, it is a pony. Do people drop off ponies, abandon them like they do dogs? Nobody has ponies nearby. Where could he have come from? Do you suppose someone just dumped him out at the road? Even bigger question, what am I going to do with him?"

"I never heard of people dropping off ponies," Lori said. "But you're right, there aren't any horses around here. I'm sure someone will come looking for him. He must be some kid's pet."

I let go of his halter and pushed the barn door open just enough to slip inside, rolling the entry closed behind me. My horses both stood, heads out their hay doors, wondering about the unusual commotion outside the barn. I sent them both out the side door to the paddock, although Spirit's curiosity led him to stop on the way with his nose against the space between the wall and the door, his nostrils flaring to capture the new smell. He put his head in the air, nose up, lip curled. The big gray gelding pushed against the wood with his nose, rattling the door before moving on outside. Kirby, our sixteen-hand chestnut, just headed for the round bale, more focused on breakfast than on the visitor.

I retrieved a lead rope from the tack room and returned to Black Pony still waiting outside the barn. I snapped the rope on his halter, and he followed me willingly into the barn. "Well, little one, you can have the big boys' stall for now." I was afraid to turn him out with my two twelve-hundred-pound quarter horses, not knowing how they might react. Kirby could be a pasture bully. The pony sniffed around the stall, nibbling on a bit of leftover hay, took a sip from the water bucket, and looked at me as if waiting for direction. Scratching his neck, I could feel his already thick coat of winter hair preparing for coming frigid days in the Upper Peninsula of Michigan. I assured him we would find his owners.

Lori and I headed back to the house so I could begin my search for where the black pony had come from. Where was his home? I was sure someone was desperate. I knew how I would feel if one of my boys were missing. I made a mental list of how to proceed. The animal shelter, my first call. Then the local radio station. I would email all my friends who had horses, find out who had ponies. I stopped at the base of the steps to the house and looked around at the surroundings—dense forest, river, sparse population. *How did the pony get here?*

Lori said her goodbyes and wished me luck in finding the pony's home.

My first two calls only netted an opportunity to leave a message and instructions on how to get an event on the radio. I sent a quick email to anyone I thought might have a lead, updated my husband on the situation, and headed out to make personal contacts. I drove to town, my first stop the animal shelter. As I explained the circumstances to three wide-eyed volunteers at the shelter, I sensed their concern: Was I about to give them a pony? I assured them I would care for the pony for now but needed their assistance in finding the owner. I gave them my contact information and a description of the black pony.

On to the radio station, where I filled out a form and was promised it would be read on Telephone Time, known to locals as TT, the holy grail of communication. This nine-to-noon show every day provided a forum for people to buy and sell anything or make announcements of local interest. I did remember once hearing a woman describe her missing mule, so I was sure there might be an answer here.

A couple of leads from emails regarding people with ponies were dead ends. Their ponies were all accounted for, peacefully grazing in their pastures. No home for Black Pony. No desperate owner looking for a beloved lost pet.

It was well past midday when I returned home. Late October days meant the sun would drop below the horizon within the hour, darkness coming earlier each day. Our horses stood at the gate outside the barn door. Rarely did they spend a night outside. Bears, wolves, and coyotes were prevalent in the woods surrounding the paddock. If not a direct threat, they did cause the horses to be very agitated when dusk came.

Tonight, however, they would need to surrender their barn to Black Pony, the visitor. I fed and watered all three and called to the dog as I walked toward the house. Kaiser, our German Shorthaired Pointer, bounded in the door ahead of me, announcing our arrival.

I apprised my husband: no home for pony yet. Before I went to bed that night, I took a flashlight and the dog and walked out to the barn to check on Black Pony. He was lying down in the corner of the big stall, half buried in shavings. He seemed so small as I watched, blinking his eyes as the light shone in the stall. I walked around the barn to check on the horses and gave them a treat to make up for their spending the night outside.

After a fitful night's sleep spent worrying about the horses and Black Pony, I got out of bed. As I poured a cup of morning coffee, darkness still shrouded the woods around our house. I opened my laptop, expecting to find an email claiming the black pony. Nothing. Not a single clue to ownership. I looked out the window to the dark forest and once again wondered how this little animal had found his way through the woods. How had he safely arrived at our barn? Why wasn't someone desperate to find him?

My husband walked into the kitchen, reaching for the coffeepot. "Did you solve the mystery?"

"No." I slumped forward, elbows resting on the kitchen butcher block island, eyes closing. It had now been twenty-four hours since the wayward traveler arrived.

"Well?"

I sat straight up on the stool, reacting to his tone, anticipating the coming question.

"What are you going to do? We have a barn with two stalls and no room for another animal." He poured his coffee, adding a touch of cream, and sat next to me at the counter, his arm around my shoulder. He took a quick look down the river, a morning ritual, always hoping to spot wildlife crossing the shallows downstream. I knew if he were feeling better, it would not be such a concern. It would be something we could solve together.

After breakfast I walked to the barn. Black Pony stretched his neck to look over the stall wall and then nickered to me. "Well, my little friend, if you are spending another day with us, you're going to have to get to know the big boys." He stood still as I brushed his coat and combed burrs from his mane. Black Pony's hair was thick like a black bear ready to sleep for the winter. His dark eyes glistened as he watched me. There was not a white hair on his body. He reminded me of a tiny version of the horse I had growing up. Queen was a coal-black mare, the horse I had from the time I was nine years old until she died at age thirty plus. She was sweet and gentle, just like this pony.

"You can't spend such a beautiful day inside." I rolled the stall door open and clipped the lead rope on his halter. "Let's go meet the big boys." I led him out in the paddock. My horses moved to surround him; they were so much bigger that he could have ducked under their bellies. Bravely, Black Pony stretched his neck to be nose to nose, first with Spirit and then Kirby. He was like the new kid on the playground who was happy to be included in a kickball game. For the remainder of the day, he was next to one of the horses, almost leaning against them. There seemed to be an understanding. The big boys were being very patient with their newfound friend.

More days passed; no owner claimed the pony. I continued to circulate emails to anyone who might know where this pony belonged. When I opened my laptop the morning of day five, I was certain a message from the owner would be there. Still nothing. I sat on the steps of the back porch, head in my hands, staring at my dusty boots. What would I do if no claim was made?

I walked to the barn, kicking rocks in the gravel. I threw a stick for the dog. A raven screeched a warning. I leaned on the fence, my boot propped on the bottom rail. I watched Black Pony. He had walked so far to get here, through woods, swamps, who knows what else. He shadowed the big horses everywhere. For now, Black Pony was happy and safe. He had found a home and was settling in. He had been rescued.

We remained Black Pony's foster family for almost three weeks until one morning a message arrived: "We are searching for our granddaughter's pony lost three weeks earlier."

We learned Black Pony had traveled over ten miles on his journey to visit us. We were sorry to see our little friend leave. But we were happy he was reunited with his family.

12

Horse Calling

Andi Lehman

The spotlight on the corner of our patio cast a yellow path through the pre-dawn darkness. I watched my adult daughter, Reyn, stroll through the dewy grass toward the barn. Soft whuffles from her pony, Proper, and a sharp whinny from the exuberant Arabian, Aslan, harmonized with the stirring songbirds. Our miniature horse, Pumpkin, added his high-pitched neigh like a merry descant to the melodic mix.

Reyn flipped on the barn lights, illuminating her four friends. In addition to Proper, Aslan, and Pumpkin, the big Appaloosa, Strider, waited restlessly—the least vocal and confident of her private herd. Her faithful silhouette moved easily from stall to stall, murmuring tender greetings I couldn't see or hear but knew by heart. From the time she was old enough to recognize a horse, Reyn had heard them calling.

When Reyn was a toddler, her favorite animals in board books were horses, ponies, zebras, and unicorns. She loved to answer the question, "What's a horse say?" and she squealed with joy in her car seat if we passed one grazing by the roadside or gracing a local sign. When we visited my parents, the first thing we had to do was pet their neighbor's aging geldings.

In stores, Reyn could find a Breyer horse or My Little Pony like an equine bloodhound. She discovered C. W. Anderson's Billy and Blaze books at the public library, and we read aloud the whole series. She knew the names of all the Disney horses (much more interesting to her than the princes or princesses who rode them), and she knew the breed and traits of every steed.

By her fourth birthday, Reyn could trot on all fours as well as she could run. She pranced around the living room, tossing her long blond hair around her shoulders and snorting as she pawed the carpet beneath her. The dog gate between our living room and den morphed into a high jump, and she sailed over it regularly while I worried about the development of the bones in her legs.

At the playground, she enjoyed circling the sand pit on her hands and feet to demonstrate a perfect walk, trot, canter, and gallop. Other parents and their kids met our horse-girl with astonishment. Verbally, they offered polite admiration, but I noticed the wide-eyed looks that passed between moms who no doubt labeled Reyn as "odd."

She *was* odd. No one in our family boasted an equestrian background. We didn't know a hunter from a jumper or the difference between a pony and a horse, but Reyn did—before she entered preschool. Her vocabulary brimmed with equitation terms: Morgans and mustangs, saddles and stirrups, duns and dappled grays, the art of dressage. She drank in horses like chocolate milk.

On her fifth birthday, we did two things that all responsible parents do when their children show an abiding interest in something. We gave her the opportunity to pursue it and the tools she needed to do so. First, we signed her up for lessons at a local riding barn. Second, despite the limitations in our suburb, we got her a horse.

Sort of.

The young mare was lovingly created by her dad and grandfather from a wooden sawhorse and the head of a stick pony. Reyn promptly dubbed her "Katy" after her favorite horse in the stable where she rode. Katy lived in her bedroom closet and peered at us through the open door, her chin resting on a length of yarn tacked across the entrance. Trips to the thrift store provided the appropriate equipment and fake feed that Reyn gave to Katy twice a day, every day.

We settled into a routine with our horse-crazed kiddo—regular lessons and occasional youth shows—your basic English equitation fare. The whole thing mystified her dad and me. We couldn't imagine where this horse-drawn life might take her, but we agreed to lope alongside for the duration.

One morning as Reyn and I walked through the big barn where she trained, she stopped short in her dusty Ariat riding boots and put her hand on my arm.

"Do you smell that?" she asked.

I smelled a lot of things. Hay and horse manure, mostly, not my first choice of aromas. Before I could answer, she continued.

"That's the best smell in the world," she said.

Too dumbfounded to reply, I just returned her smile.

A few days after Reyn started kindergarten, our family was invited to attend a local rodeo with acquaintances who were competing in the events. True to form, she begged at the first break to meet the horses. Our hosts led her toward the arena while we stopped by a vendor to purchase drinks. At the sound of some commotion in the big round corral, I looked up to see a large horse tearing around the enclosure with a small child on his back. Our child. Her feet couldn't reach the stirrups, and she had lost the reins. In what seemed to me a hideous slow motion, she fell from the huge Western saddle onto the dirt surface, landed in a clump, and lay still. By the time we got to her, she sat in a daze—shaking, crying, and bleeding.

The distraught horse owner fluttered around us, stammering apologies and repeating, "I thought she could ride!" I stifled my angry reply as we checked Reyn for bone breaks and basic cognitive function. When we were satisfied that she could walk and talk, her dad lifted her in his arms, and we drove to the nearest emergency room.

Two X-rays and a brain scan later, the doctor released us to go home. Reyn suffered multiple cuts and bruises and a fractured nose (which still features a knotty reminder). The following day, both her eyes turned black like a prize boxer's. We thought her journey with horses was over.

We should have known better.

Despite her ordeal, she refused to miss her riding lesson (which she used to pet and groom her mount) and demanded to know when she would be allowed to ride again. Her teacher smiled at my amazement, but she understood our daughter. The horses were still calling.

Reyn clambered back in the saddle, and we trotted along for a while without incident—until her dad and I decided to live on one salary and downsize our home. Since we had to move anyway, we ventured into the countryside in a neighboring state. We traded our big two-story house with a tiny yard for a little ranch-style home with acreage.

And an old wooden barn.

Now ten, Reyn researched the cost of buying and keeping a real horse. She presented a shoestring budget plan to us, and we promised to consider it as soon as she could clean out the ancient stalls and find a mount at a reasonable price.

But all horse owners know there's no such thing as a cheap one. Show animals are expensive. We talked to several people selling their chargers for serious money and concluded that if God wanted Reyn to have a ride of her own, he would have to provide it.

He did.

Through the hippotherapy club where Reyn volunteered, we learned about a rejected perennial broodmare who needed a home. When she "dropped" a solid-colored foal instead of a multi-colored paint, her owner declared her usefulness over because she failed to produce what he expected. He sold her at auction to our colleagues, who discovered she panicked around swinging ropes. Obviously abused in her past, the pony needed someone with time and patience to give her a new life.

The breeder had called her "Prop Wash." I knew the word from my father, a retired aircraft carrier pilot. As a part of the hazing process, seasoned fliers often instructed new recruits to locate the fictitious cleaning fluid and scrub the propellors. Prop wash is the "dirty" or disrupted air and wind that flows over the wings and through a plane's propellor in flight. Either way, I thought it a derogatory name to give a filly.

Despite the moniker, Reyn fell in love with Prop Wash, and on her eleventh birthday, she acquired the fourteen-year-old paint for a pittance. The beautiful auburn pony sported four white socks, a white blaze, and a white patch on her belly. She stood twelve hands high, and she seemed to have a quiet spirit. But many introverted horses harbor an explosive side. Our new resident remained calm only if she was left alone.

As soon as Reyn asked Prop Wash to do anything—take a bit, accept a saddle, or change gaits from a walk—she met with resistance, which is natural and correctible in mistreated horses, but we didn't know that. In a few short months, hope dissolved into fear as Reyn battled daily with a rearing red and white dragon on the end of her reins.

Well-meaning folks said we expected too much, too soon. Others said we expected too little. Reyn needed to be firmer; she needed to be gentler. She should completely break the horse and then rebuild her. But what if the process broke them both? We hired a local trainer, but the more demanding the lessons, the more violent the response. The trainer recommended we consider a different horse.

Meanwhile, Reyn spent hours researching training theories and fundamentals. Desperate to bond with Prop Wash, she read every available book on equine behavior only to find herself mired in conflicting information. Without the skills or the savvy to make appropriate changes, we all thought rider and pony were at an impasse.

Once again, we were wrong.

Reyn heard about a natural horsemanship program that emphasized the way horses communicate as the means to reach them. If we can learn their language, we can access their minds—that was the premise. We attended a local two-day event and were stunned by the transformation we saw in the "problem" horses presented each morning. Reyn bought the first set in a series of training courses, and she went to work.

It helped that her own energy around animals and people is naturally low and tranquil. But the program taught her how to read her pony's emotions and when and how to be assertive rather than aggressive. As weeks passed, the pair established a connection. Reyn invested her money and effort in something she realized could change her relationship with not just one horse but all horses.

She attended multiple clinics with Proper Partner, renamed to represent their new positive goals. They drew the attention of the renowned instructor under whom Reyn studied. Within two years, Reyn and Proper joined the presentation team performing for the organization at regional events.

But the occasion that showed how far pony and girl had come together took place in a high-ceilinged, glass mall structure that housed a popular network television talk show. Proper and Reyn and her instructor were to arrive at 8:30 a.m. for an interview and demonstration in the multileveled atrium studio.

I knew Proper Partner had an amazing trust in Reyn, built from hours of learning to understand each other. But as soon as we pulled into the downtown parking lot, I spotted our first obstacle. Once we crossed the busy city street, we would reach the entrance to the huge building—clear, double sliding doors that opened automatically when sensing movement. What would our pony make of this unexpected challenge, and how would Reyn lead her across the menacing threshold?

Proper followed her with confidence across the six-lane road, over the curb, and onto the sidewalk in front of the big doors. Reyn gave her a moment to take them in. They watched a couple of people enter the mall and listened to the swooshing noise made by the glass panels. To the diminutive mare, the entryway must have looked like a hungry mouth opening and closing, ready to gobble up unsuspecting equines.

Reyn waited for the pony to blow out a little air and relax before extending her arm with the lead rope toward the doors. As soon as Proper felt the slight movement and saw where Reyn was directing her gaze, she stepped forward. The mechanical maw yawned open, and they entered the atrium side by side.

We spread a tarp down at the filming area to calm the fears of the nervous and excited crew who assumed a horse "accident" must be imminent. I was more concerned that the amplified sound in the big building would spook Proper into calling out for the safety of other horses. I forgot that Reyn *was* her safety and her leader, a position earned with consistent effort and great instruction.

Proper Partner never made a sound. She stood relaxed, her tail barely moving. She kept one eye on Reyn while she surveyed the new world unfolding before her. The venue was brightly lit by special equipment and screens. Two huge cameras on wheels faced the interview area, and the sounds of voices, machinery, and shoes scrabbling on the tiled surface echoed all around us. The strong smell of coffee and donuts from the corner cafe hung over the atrium like a sweet fog.

Reyn ran her hands over Proper's withers and leaned into the brushed and shiny coat to breathe in her favorite scent. Three, two, one, and we were live. The morning show host introduced Reyn's popular instructor and asked her several questions about the training program. He shifted attention to Proper and Reyn, and they performed several tasks on command to demonstrate the effectiveness of their communication skills.

Proper Partner yielded to pressure from her front and hind quarters. She politely raised her hoof for inspection when Reyn asked with a subtle gesture. She flexed her neck laterally on both sides. And, to the surprise of the crew, she never had an accident—not one.

Thousands of local viewers and horse program followers tuned in to watch. But the real excitement happened after the fact when so many natural horsemanship students from around the world tried to stream the recorded show that they crashed the television station's website.

That day, an unwanted broodmare and a persistent girl demonstrated what is possible between horses and humans—a trusting relationship that bridges two species and benefits both. Reyn and her rescued pony had learned to speak a language older than Xenophon, a language based on mutual respect and love.

Now, as I watched Reyn filling water buckets from the barn spigot, my eyes misted in memories. I recalled her standing on Proper's back with her arms stretched up to the sky, riding bridle-less and bareback with her fingers laced through Aslan's mane, sitting on the ground while all four horses trotted around her in a circle like planets orbiting the sun. I thought of Proper Partner, almost thirty-six years old and blind in both eyes but still respon-sive to Reyn's touch or her voice. Her charges were silent as they enjoyed their morning hay and grain.

But the horses would speak to her again, and Reyn would con-tinue to hear them and reply. When the God of second chances calls us for a purpose, he also equips us to do the work.

Even when he calls with a whinny.

13

The Abandoned Foal Turned Inspiration

Nicole M. Miller

It was the summer of fresh faces at the barn. I'd been working almost every day while taking lessons and showing my horse on the weekends. The hours were long, the manure was ripe, and my muscles were constantly sore.

But then two new baby foals arrived, and the barn staff all lost their collective minds over these two darling new residents.

One was Cash, a dark bay, stunning from the start. He overshadowed all and obviously had a rich career ahead of him. The other was pitifully named Grunnion (a type of small fish) as a play off his sire's name, Gunner. He was a straggly, knobby-kneed little guy. Not quite the looker that his lineage would predict. His coloring was patchy—we expected he'd be gray, and yet his fur lacked the luster and finesse of his peers. He had large hooves for a foal his size, and his ears were lopsided and disproportionate. He looked more like a character from a Dr. Seuss book than a fine, purebred Arabian.

Unfortunately, his dam, Pye, rejected little Grunnion right from the start, gnashing her teeth and biting at him and anyone who came in the stall. She took a chunk out of my arm that required a tetanus shot. So out came the horse-sized baby bottle and the line of barn staffers to help raise the rejected foal.

Despite his rough entry into the world, little Grunnion proved to be a friendly and amiable little guy, taking after his sire and not after his mother. He relied on us for food and comfort and trusted us without question.

It was a summer I will never forget. Despite all the stalls I cleaned and horses I groomed, I'd do it all over again for that little ugly duckling of a colt. I'd never known a horse from such an early age, and it was a joy to watch him grow and learn everything about the world. But time passed, and the years drifted by. Grunnion grew from his bottle feedings and moved into a pasture with his half-brother, Cash.

In my senior year of high school, Grunnion was a spunky little two-year-old at the barn with no owner and no real future. He was still straggly and knobby-kneed. The trainer had no intention of showing him, so he wanted to find Grunnion a home where he could be a trail horse or pasture buddy.

I'd been showing on the Arabian breed circuit but knew that trajectory was due to switch course as I went into college and adulthood. I was selling my main show horse, Sigi, and as I talked to my trainer, he mentioned that he'd be giving Grunnion away to a good home.

Instantly, I raised my hand.

I'd helped raise Grunnion. He was the last progeny of Gunner, the distinguished stud at the barn that I'd worked with and adored. It didn't make sense for me to take on an untrained two-year-old right before going away to college, but I couldn't leave this horse behind. We were connected.

Over the next few years, the little awkward two-year-old grew out of his high withers and grew into his large head. His knees picked up when he trotted, and that ugly duckling had turned into a beautiful swan. My trainer later admitted he hadn't seen that side of Grunnion before, and he might have made a great show horse after all.

But this little treasure was all mine.

Best of all, he grew into an even more unique personality.

One summer day, my younger brother and sister accidentally kicked their soccer ball into the pasture, and Grunnion playfully ran after it and nuzzled it, then pawed at it with his hoof. A new game was formed, and Grunnion eagerly chased the ball each time we chucked it into the pasture.

Grunnion also made a surprise entrance into one of my big interests outside of horse showing. Since I was sixteen, I'd been working on writing a novel based on one of the most inspirational horse stories I'd read. After the Nazis stole high-bred horses from all over Europe during World War II, a contingent of Patton's Third Army went into occupied territory and evacuated hundreds of horses from the clutches of the Russians.

I'd been crafting a novel based on these events. Then I learned through researching Grunnion's bloodlines that my horse was a descendant of Witez II, a horse rescued by the American army and brought over to the United States in 1946.

Grunnion was not only the most personable and spunky horse I'd known, but he turned out to be a piece of this history I'd been obsessing over for years.

We've been together twenty-two years now and counting. Grunnion has followed me through college, marriage, career transitions, and several moves. He's been ridden by my husband and two young kids, and he's been fawned over by countless Arabian horse lovers for his classic looks and historic lineage.

Grunnion still runs up to you when called, and he's still known to kick a soccer ball around. He'd been discounted as a youth because he wasn't going to win ribbons. But he's won over countless hearts, from my family members to my future husband.

We're bonded, and we're inseparable. He's meant more to me than I could have ever anticipated and has had a "hoof" in nearly every part of my life.

And it all started one summer when the little ugly duckling of a foal plopped into my lap. He's brought me joy and inspiration and laughter time and time again, and I know he will do so for years and years to come.

Sometimes the most unique gifts come in the strangest of packages. Grunnion taught me that beauty and value are more than what you see on the surface. And even the strange, unfortunate name of "Grunnion" doesn't determine one's destiny. Grunnion, my little fish and little companion, has left a mark beyond what anyone might have expected twenty-two years ago.

14

Cosmo

Fay Odeh

I love animals. But I didn't grow up with them. I was raised in Palestine, not far from Jerusalem, in a hot, dry land, and I came to the United States when I was eighteen to be with my husband, Steve. Before that, Steve had moved to the States as a single man, then moved back to Palestine to find a wife. I fell in love with him the first time I saw him. I told all my girlfriends that he was the man I wanted to marry.

Happily, we did marry. Steve moved back to the States in Michigan, and I followed six months later. The terrain and the climate in Michigan were very different for us after Palestine. But we both came to love the four seasons, which are especially enjoyable in this state. And we came to enjoy animals in our life.

After we lived in the Detroit area for a time, we bought forty acres of a former cattle ranch. We moved to the country where we raised some Angus beef and a few horses, one or two at a time. We bought and ran a family-style restaurant in a town nearby, and we sometimes used our own beef for the meat choices. I was having my children during these years, and some of the kids and I learned to ride our horses, Western style. I loved every minute of it—both raising my eight children and riding the horses.

We bought Cosmo from a friend. Cosmo was a purebred Arabian stallion, all white except for a small gray mark on his nose. He was tall, beautiful, and majestic. I fell in love with him right away, and the wonderful thing was that this gorgeous animal loved me back. He was so happy when I was with him. Cosmo's whole demeanor would brighten when I approached. He would make nickering and snorting noises in happiness. He would tuck his head under my arm, as calm as anything. I rode him a lot, and he was always gentle, always kind.

Until a man tried to ride him, that is. Cosmo didn't like men, and we never understood why. He tried rubbing male riders off with the fence. Sometimes he even threw them off. One of my sons received a minor injury from Cosmo trying to dislodge him. This horse simply did not want a male to ride his back. Since four of my children were male—not to mention my husband—this was a problem. They rode Cosmo, but it was always a struggle.

But I certainly didn't have that problem. Cosmo seemed to like me riding him as much as I liked riding him. For me, having Cosmo was like having another baby, the way he would want to cuddle up against me, letting me cradle his mighty head. He was my pet, and I so enjoyed him. I can never forget how rewarding it felt to have a creature that majestic nuzzled under my arm.

But Cosmo was a complicated horse.

One night in a cold December, my nineteen-year-old son, Tariq, decided to take a moonlit ride on Cosmo. There was lots of snow and a full moon—perfect for a quiet ride. Around midnight, everyone was in bed except Tariq and me. I was doing house chores as I heard him leave the house for the barn.

An hour later, I heard a knock at the back door. I assumed it was Tariq, but it was a neighbor. She had been driving home from her night shift job when she saw what appeared like an apparition in the snow in front of my house. But it was no apparition. It was my big, white Cosmo with Tariq atop him. Together, they stood in the middle of the road. Simply standing, not moving.

The neighbor pulled up and put her window down. Tariq told her that once he and Cosmo got on the road, the horse stopped walking and decided not to move. They had been standing still in subzero weather for an hour now. No matter what Tariq tried, our strong-willed stallion would not move. Tariq said later that he thought the horse might try to buck him off. That was also part of Cosmo's personality. But fortunately, that didn't happen; Cosmo just planted himself and stood.

Our house had a quarter-mile driveway, so shouting could not alert me. Tariq could only hope someone would drive up and see them but not collide with them. My son knew he couldn't leave Cosmo out there on the road, so he simply waited on this freezing night. We were so grateful the neighbor came along and stopped.

I bundled up with coat and boots and gloves. At the barn, I grabbed some sweet feed with molasses and headed down the long driveway. There was a tall willow tree at the end of the drive leading onto the road, and just beyond that was where Cosmo chose to stop in the road. He was not leaving home.

Once Cosmo saw me, as usual, his demeanor changed. He was always sweet and affectionate with me, and even in this odd circumstance, he immediately snuggled under my arm. I talked to him and fussed over him and gave him some feed. Then I took his harness and walked him back to the barn with no problem whatsoever.

It was time for a family discussion about this horse. We'd had Cosmo for two years, but it was clear he was an unsafe horse for everyone but me. We determined we should find him another home. Oh, I was sad to see my handsome friend go. I could only hope he would have a happy life at his next home.

A couple of years after Cosmo was rehomed, I was at the restaurant. A family was seated around a large round table, and they called me over. "We're the people who bought Cosmo," they said. I learned that, for whatever reason, he didn't have the problems with males that we had. I was so pleased to meet them and to hear them say Cosmo was a fine horse for them. He was content, they said. I felt very good about that.

Since then, my husband has passed on, and all my children have moved on to careers and marriage. I have a cat but no more horses. I enjoy other animals, though. The wildlife come to my backyard—deer, geese, sandhill cranes. A gray heron visits me every day. When the moon rises over my pond, I take pictures of it. I can't get enough.

And in the winter out there, in my mind's eye, I see my gorgeous stallion Cosmo in a full moon, standing like an elegant statue in the snow.

15

A Canter and a Kiss

Susan Friedland

When I first saw the dark bay gelding with a narrow blaze and long, bushy forelock standing in the crossties at a San Diego sales barn, my heart skipped a beat. The week before, I found this pretty horse through word of mouth. On paper he was a perfect description of what I was looking for in a riding partner, and he was in my teacher's-salary-friendly price range. I was elated!

I had been unsuccessfully horse shopping, looking for my fourth horse—one with whom I could trail ride, jump small fences, dabble in dressage, and just enjoy grooming and hand grazing. I sought my new best friend.

Four years earlier, my heart horse, DC, a twenty-three-year-old Thoroughbred, had died. Due to my life circumstances with a lengthy commute to my school and the purchase of a fixer-upper, I hadn't been in a position to bring another horse into my life. Until now.

When I took my first ride on Tiz A Knight, a retired Thoroughbred racehorse with just a few months of retraining under his belt, I was a fortysomething returning equestrian. In the wake of DC's death, I'd only had the opportunity to ride a few times, so now I was timid in the saddle. Knight's 16.3-hand frame and forward stride both intimidated me and made me feel secure. My previous mount was the same size and build. Knight could have been a stunt double for DC, although DC's blaze looked like a backward question mark and Knight's a medieval sword. The instant I swung my right leg over the saddle and settled into its deepest part, I felt at home.

Walking Knight around to the left, then right, then circling around colorful jumps in the arena was a thrill reminiscent of my first time riding a horse solo. When I was about ten years old, my sister's friend brought her pinto over to our house and invited me to ride. I sat tall in the Western saddle that day. After a quick lesson on steering, I used my heel to urge the horse forward. The black and white mare and I cruised around our tulip tree and then the red maple. For a shy bookworm of a girl, sitting so high above the earth was life changing. Once in the saddle, I didn't want to leave. It was better than Narnia or an amusement park!

Now I picked up the laced reins shorter and lightly squeezed my calves along Knight's barrel. He launched into a perky trot. I rose up and down in rhythm as he maintained his relaxed stride down the long side of the arena.

That day I was too timid to canter. I worried I'd ruin this beautiful horse because of my too-long riding hiatus. What business did a middle-aged re-rider have riding a former elite athlete?

"Ride him like he's yours," the seller urged.

And so I did, which meant I wasn't flopping around too tragically. We walked and trotted, skipping the canter. I knew if Knight cleared his pre-purchase exam, we'd have many days together to canter.

The vet check went well, and canter we did!

My new horse was the best. We rode dusty trails, had lessons a couple times a week, and competed at a few local horse shows. We once rode in a clinic with a former Olympic jumping coach. It was both terrifying and exhilarating as he barked out orders and made me canter a course more complex than I ever thought I was capable of.

One time Knight was even a model for a friend of a friend who wanted to do a knight and maiden photoshoot. He was paid for his time and good looks as a beautiful redhead in a flowy dress and her handsome boyfriend in a knight's suit kissed under a sycamore tree with Knight as a backdrop.

A few years into owning Knight, a Southern California wildfire enveloped the equestrian center where Knight lived. All seventy horses were evacuated safely, but I saw the barn where Knight had been stalled hours earlier in flames on the local evening news. Other evacuees and I were welcomed to a nearby farm while the damaged equestrian center was rebuilt.

Knight and I continued to train and were still trying to work on smoothing out our jumping. His jump was big, larger than necessary, for the teeny fences we faced. I felt insecure when he dashed at a crossrail as though it were an imposing steeplechase jump. I got nervous. The more nervous I got, the quicker he'd go. Aside from jumping being a challenge, riding on the flat was lovely.

One Saturday morning as I was tacking up for a lesson, my sweet bay boy pinned his ears as I walked toward him with the saddle. He wielded a mean face. The angry look stopped me in my tracks, and the saddle didn't go on that day. Or the next. Or the one following that. Something wasn't right with my horse.

The veterinarian came out to discover what was ailing him, and the first diagnosis was a nebulous "wind-up." His back was sore. She prescribed a drug, and Knight received acupuncture, laser therapy, hand walking, and stall rest. He made only mild improvements. At some point we decided to radiograph his back. That's when things got interesting.

The veterinarian had a hardcover textbook from her vet school days and quietly paged over to a picture of an X-ray. "This is a horse's spine."

I nodded, noticing the white fence posts of mostly vertical vertebrae. I could see the horse's withers like a gently sloping mountain.

She opened her laptop and showed an X-ray of a spine that looked like fallen dominoes. Vertebrae were leaning on each other, with minimal space between them. "This is your horse's spine. He has overriding dorsal spinous processes, also known as 'kissing spine,'" she said.

It was obvious, even to my uneducated eye, that something was wrong with my horse's back. I tried to sound calm as I processed this new, unwelcome information. "What does this mean for him?"

The vet went on with some talk about making the best decision for my horse. As I processed this blow, the words "walking," "light work only," and "surgery" stuck with me despite my note-taking on a legal pad. My trainer watched me. The vet waited. I did not want them to see me cry.

"I'm a horse lover first and an equestrian second," I said. "I will do right by my horse."

The reality of Knight's situation hit like an anvil the next morning. I cried all day. I wept realizing my poor horse had been in pain, probably for a long time, and I had been oblivious to it. I was crushed. I would never, ever want to do anything bad to him, and I had been riding around having a wonderful time while he was not. Knight had dutifully carried me safely, even when he was uncomfortable. I promised him I would do right by him, whatever that meant.

It was evident both from what was said and what was unsaid in the following weeks that my trainer did not foresee a hopeful future for my horse. I got the sense she wanted me to move on with a different horse, but that was out of the question.

I processed my pain by writing and asking questions. I wrote a blog post titled "The Worst Possible Kiss for Your Horse: Kissing Spine," and a number of fellow horse people commented with their experiences with kissing spine. I found a Facebook group dedicated to owners of horses with kissing spine and followed along with the progress and posts of horse people just like me who also received the dreaded diagnosis.

Surgeries are available for horses like Knight, I learned. Thanks to my blog post, a friend messaged me to say her mare had just had the kissing spine surgery and was doing great. She said they were about to compete in their first three-day event. I showed Knight's X-rays to a family friend, an equine chiropractor, and he wasn't alarmed. He said there were training techniques to strengthen Knight's back. I sent the X-rays to my former trainer's vet, and as a favor he looked at them. He said my horse would benefit from injections. If that didn't work, surgery was an option.

I needed time to keep researching and processing the next steps for my horse. That summer I was set to be in Europe for three weeks. I decided to send Knight to a new farm about an hour and a half from our boarding stable right before I left on vacation. We could both enjoy downtime while apart. The big bonus to this farm—in addition to access to an aqua treadmill and the owner's skills as a horse physical therapist—was the acres of green pastures, a rarity in Southern California.

During my initial meeting with the owner and the farm tour, she told me she had worked with other horses with kissing spine. She explained that the trick was to help them develop a strong topline by encouraging them to use their core. She didn't seem to think my horse's situation was a retirement sentence. "I have a horse with kissing spine who competes in meter twenty jumpers." She sent me home with fresh eggs from her chicken coop and a hope-filled outlook.

I hired a shipper, and my bay boy went for a summer vacation. For one month, he got to chill and graze with the San Jacinto Mountains in the distance. After a bone scan at a sport horse specialty veterinary hospital, Knight was slowly introduced back into work. From my hotel in Munich, I spoke with the young veterinarian who conducted the bone scan. She explained in detail how my horse's body looked, and she concluded with this statement: "For the level of work you want to pursue with your horse, he should be fine. If an injection and conservative approaches don't work, he is a candidate for surgery." A weight was lifted.

A few weeks after my return from Europe, Knight received his first injection treatment. I was able to ride my horse for the first time in months. He was happy and relaxed. I cantered, and the joy returned. This was a win, but it also meant he was ready to be my riding horse again, and I would need to find a new farm.

I had read of an upper-level eventer who had a horse with kissing spine, and part of the lifestyle choice she had made was for him to be in a field 24/7. Grazing and reaching the head and neck down, she believed, was helpful for improving musculature for a strong back.

Two months earlier I had ridden in a mock fox hunt. A trusty solid bay gelding expertly carried me around a ranch with a dramatic mountain backdrop that was used for the opening credits of the television show *Bonanza*. The pine groves and open grasslands scattered with cattle and sage enchanted me.

The warmth of the Master of Foxhounds, an old-school horseman and walking equine encyclopedia, drew me into the sport. This man with a white mustache and a twinkle in his eyes had done everything from training racehorses to working cattle to polo and eventing. He also owned a sport horse breeding farm with big fields.

I shared with him and his young trainer about my horse's diagnosis. They were unbothered. The trainer said they had a few horses with kissing spine who were eventing (and at higher levels than my timid self would ever aspire to).

I asked if they had any open spots for boarders, and the answer was yes! The horse farm was seventy miles from my home, through Orange County and Los Angeles traffic. But I was willing to make the drive so my horse could live his best life.

The day of Knight's move to the new farm with the seasoned horseman and the kind young trainer was drama-free. He hopped up into the trailer for the ride to his new home. Upon unloading, he immediately put his head down and vacuumed up bits of alfalfa from a nearby hay bale as we awaited his pasture assignment. There were no whinnies, no wide-eyed looks. Knight acted as if he had lived at this farm his whole life. He was comfortable, which made me comfortable.

Knight began to thrive at his new horse farm with hours and hours of turnout in a field with friends and training by an open-minded eventer. A fellow boarder later revealed to me that when the farm owner, the Master of Foxhounds, first saw Knight, he was "giddy." He appreciated a well-bred Thoroughbred, and he thought my horse, even with a kissing spine diagnosis, was a fine animal.

The young trainer began working with Knight on both basic dressage and over fences. She showed me certain stretches and exercises I could do to help Knight's back, continuing with the principles the physical therapist had taught us. Knight's chiropractor at the new barn said, "Ride the horse, not the X-rays."

And so I did. With the support of my new barn family, Knight and I rode in a dressage schooling show and participated in a cross-country clinic, jumping small wooden fences and up and down banks. We even went fox hunting at the ranch several times. The pack of hounds did not faze Knight, nor did the Western movie terrain of undulating flats, cacti, rocky hills, and dry riverbeds.

After one fox hunt (which really is a coyote chase with the intent to shoo away the wily predators from calves), I chatted with a barn friend. She had not ridden in the hunt that day but had galloped racehorses as a young woman. Proudly I gushed, "I can't believe how good Knight was. I've only ridden him in groomed arenas and on well-cleared trails. We trotted and cantered over changing terrain, up and down, into the dry riverbed and out. It was like he already knew how to do that."

"Not surprising for a smart, athletic Thoroughbred to be careful and navigate like that," she said.

I smiled. I was proud of my beautiful horse with a heart of gold who then, and to this day, takes care of me with every canter stride, even with his less-than-perfect spine. Despite his anatomy, he always has my back.

16

Reno's Legacy

Barbara Ellin Fox

"Mom, there's a BLM horse adoption in Flagstaff this weekend."

The Bureau of Land Management (BLM) held adoptions for captured wild horses throughout the Southwest. The adoption events had been too far away to bother with, especially since I'd been told the horses lacked quality.

"Can we go? It's at the feed store."

Since I'm an advocate for learning something new and we lived in Flagstaff, I could hardly say no. "But we're not adopting a wild horse," I said.

"I know, but can't we just go see them?"

I should've known better than to give in to my adult daughter, Alisha. Long ago, we banned her from visiting animal shelters. She always found that special dog in need of a home.

But soon we found ourselves parking in front of the feed store and wandering behind the building. Snorts of horses and the odor of fresh manure had transformed the small business into a gallery of wild horses. We walked through an aisle dividing a dozen small pens set against the backdrop of a huge livestock semi and San Francisco Peaks.

Each pen contained three to five horses or burros. Dust puffed from the hooves of a tall, older mare who paced with gaunt flanks as if she'd not drunk water, something common with a nervous horse. Even domestic horses stress over travel to a strange place. Strain showed in the younger wild horses through listless eyes and drooped heads. Only a few curious creatures watched as we moved from pen to pen. Periodically, a metal panel clanked when an aggressive horse threatened a timid one.

Some horses had globs of winter hair hanging from their bellies and dreadlocks in their mane or sections of their manes rubbed out. All the horses had scrapes and minor injuries, and some had a slight discharge from their nostrils. As a group, though, they showed more quality and balance than I'd expected. The colorful coats of roans and buckskins were sure to draw attention. In the end pens, cute burros with enormous eyes and long ears peeked between the panel slats. Every animal had a thin rope around its neck with a plastic ID tag, and all had brands.

We perused the pens while discussing who might adopt a wild horse in Flagstaff. Few people viewed the horses. One or two Native American families from the nearby Navajo and Hopi reservations congregated around the mare pens, and three boys from Teen Challenge tried hard to get the burros to eat hay from their hands.

We'd planned to learn about mustangs, not to adopt a horse. With eight of our own at home, today we'd mill around as sightseers and tire-kickers. But on our second tour around the pens, Alisha pointed out a yearling she liked. Number 1007 might have passed for a Thoroughbred, and he drew us to his pen multiple times. Not because he acknowledged us, which he didn't, but because Alisha admired his long legs, elegant neck, and pretty head, and he seemed calmer than most. Four white stockings and a blaze stood out against his walnut bay coat. Cowboys call those white markings "chrome."

There is a huge disconnect between the Bureau of Land Management and the horse-loving public. In 1971, Congress passed the Wild Free-Roaming Horse and Burro Act, declaring that "wild free-roaming horses and burros are living symbols of the historic and pioneer spirit of the West; that they contribute to the diversity of life forms within the Nation and enrich the lives of the American people; and that these horses and burros are fast disappearing from the American scene" (Public Law 92–195). Horse lovers want to see the horses live their lives in the wild.

But the BLM, tasked with managing and protecting the horses, is pressured by two industries that are subsidized by the American taxpayer. One industry wants the land's fodder to graze millions of cattle and sheep. The other industry wants the water for mining. The public is told the horses are starving or dying of thirst and need to be removed. Because they gather thousands of these wild animals, there is not the time or talent among BLM agents to treat the horses gently.

I asked a man with BLM embroidered on his shirt why most of the horses in the pens had jagged edges and chips on their hooves, while others appeared polished. He shifted his jeans at the waist. "Well, ma'am, we put those horses in a squeeze chute, tied their feet down, and sanded the hooves off with a power tool."

The image made my stomach squirm. BLM adoptions should display a banner saying "If you can't handle the answer, don't ask the question."

I don't know when we transitioned from lookie-loos to potential adopters, but we climbed into the Jeep with an application and an information booklet in hand. We debated the qualities of our favorite horses on the short drive home. Of course, this was a theoretical conversation since we had no plans to adopt.

Later that afternoon, unable to stay away, we returned to the adoption center for another perusal. Number 1007 still stood out to Alisha. At twenty-three years old, Alisha had thirteen years of experience with the United States Pony Club and two years in England with the British Horse Society. Although her interest lay with our big Thoroughbreds and event horses, I trusted her horsewoman's eye and judgement. If we adopted a wild horse, he would be my project, and #1007's size suited me.

By the next day, we'd grown attached to #1007. My resistance to adoption had held up overnight about as good as an ice cream cone in an Arizona summer. We returned to the center two hours before the scheduled bidding.

The horses acted differently this day. The older ones milled around in the pens, looking toward the mountains and ignoring people who evaluated them. Youngsters huddled together. The sharp odor of sweat, urine, and horse manure now reeked. Did the horses know their lives were about to change again?

The discharge from #1007's nose had gotten worse since yesterday, and the horses' continual movement in the pens coated the slime with dirt. I shook my head at Alisha. "I don't know about this. Do we really want a sick animal? What about our other horses?"

"We'll keep him isolated, Mom. I think we'll be fine."

The closer we got to bidding, the more we wanted to snatch "our" horse out of his cramped space and hurry him home. When crowds larger than yesterday congregated at the pens to see the horses, we feigned disinterest, hoping no one noticed our choice. The BLM agent announced the adoption rules at 10:40. Each pen held a clipboard for bids. The bidding started at 11:00 and lasted for thirty minutes. At 11:00, Alisha wrote $125 on #1007's clipboard.

We loitered near the bleachers, trying not to draw attention to #1007's pen, hoping we'd not lose him to a higher bidder. At 11:30, only a single bid had been written on #1007's clipboard. We'd adopted a mustang for less than the cost of a pair of brand-name running shoes.

Twelve animals out of forty-five received homes. The one adopted burro stayed in Flagstaff, and nine horses headed for the Navajo Reservation. The animals not adopted would load back into the livestock semi and relocate to a layover site, waiting. If the horses had no offer of homes after three tries, they'd go to long-term holding with thirty-eight thousand other wild horses.

When the time came to load #1007 into a stock trailer, we stood aside and held our breath while the BLM deftly separated our yearling from the others in his corral and chased him into the aisle. A handler waited for the signal to move the horse on. Next, a man chased him into the holding area at the end of the pens, then into the chute.

The horse fought to escape. My stomach tightened each time he banged or crashed into the narrow metal containment. Gnashing his teeth, #1007 lunged into the air to leap over the six-foot-high side. Failing, he assaulted the metal walls with his hind feet. A BLM agent climbed the chute from the outside and waited for the opportune moment to slip a halter on the horse. Then she unclipped the ID string from his neck. The trailer gate opened, and #1007 bolted inside. Alisha and I jumped into our Jeep and led the way home. As we pulled away from the adoption center, I choked back tears, wishing I had room for all the animals.

Ten minutes later, the scraggly yearling who entered the trailer as #1007 flew out as Reno's Legacy, in memory of his wild heritage in Nevada. He gave his shelter a bewildered gaze, sniffed the water tank, and chomped a mouthful of hay. For the first time since his capture, Reno had his own food and water and a space where he was not shoved around by another horse.

And then he got sick. Snot dropped in globs from his nose, and he wheezed so badly I worried he would die. How do you give antibiotics to an animal who didn't eat domestic horse food? The next morning, his breath roared and rattled through packed nostrils. We couldn't haul him to the vet or even have the vet come out because he wasn't halter trained. We had to do something before his health deteriorated more.

The veterinarian prescribed a powdered antibiotic. I shook fine alfalfa leaves into a bowl and added the antibiotic and a few dribbles of water to make the powder stick. I removed all his other food. What a relief when Reno ate the alfalfa mix from the bowl in my hands.

As much as I longed to pet and soothe Reno, I knew he'd meet human touch with revulsion. I imagined stroking his silky coat with my fingertips, washing his encrusted nose, doctoring the sores on his head, and scratching his back the way horses do with each other. In time, he'd feel safe in his surroundings—and with me.

I talked with him for hours every day while I cleaned his pen or sat on the ground. He'd watch from a distance, only coming close for his bowl of medicinal food. A week after Reno arrived, his cough had cleared, and he allowed me to rub the soft white marking on his forehead. I derived as much satisfaction from that minor accomplishment as I did from any championship horse show trophy I'd won.

Reno differed from other horses. He had no reason to want my attention. He'd lived through one of the most grueling, life-threatening experiences a horse can endure. His hooves stood up to galloping over sharp rocks and frozen ground in early January weather. Wild colts stay with their mothers until they are yearlings, but Reno coped with forced weaning at six months old. He managed traveling in a crowded stock truck to the processing facility where he endured a mechanical squeeze chute for vaccinations, freeze branding, tests, deworming, and gelding. He lived for five and a half months in a crowded feed lot without shelter from the wind, snow, or rain. Then on June 24, agents chased Reno into a livestock semi with forty-four other horses and burros to travel seven hundred miles from northwest Nevada to Arizona.

There is no more powerful tool for control than having your freedom jerked away. I knew that myself. Years in a past abusive relationship gave me hands-on experience with isolation from my family and friends and with control over where I went, what I ate, what I said, and how I reacted. I learned to accept force from someone who was bigger and stronger than me. Years of being told I was worthless and couldn't survive on my own and being forced to agree left me ashamed. And angry. Afterward, I lived with crippling self-doubt and emotional scars that made me afraid of people and of living with joy. Deep inside, I identified with Reno's experience and his fight to survive. Hope and trust were tough for us both.

But the hours I spent with him helped us bond, and slowly our relationship changed. We connected on a level deeper than familiarity. Reno had a lot to learn, and so did I. While he needed manners and socialization skills, I had to unlearn most of what I'd

gained from fifty years of handling domestic horses. I quit reacting and became an observer and a listener. I tuned in to Reno's
needs, and little by little, he rewarded me with trust. Instead of
tensing and moving away when I touched him, he softened and
moved toward me. When I approached his pen in the mornings,
his ears perked forward over bright eyes as if to say, "I've been
waiting for you." Like a friend, he wanted my attention. These
offerings gave me confidence, healed wounds, and showed me a
unique beauty as his personality blossomed.

Reno still reacts like a wild horse, and he always will. The first
time a cat crept through the barn, he startled like he'd seen a small
mountain lion. From the beginning, Reno needed to investigate
and inspect things until he knew they were safe. Even today, he
wants to know what grooming tool I intend to use to brush him.

He accepts discipline but not violence. For instance, if he misbe-
haves on the way to the paddock, rather than yell at him, I return
him to his stall. The next time, he walks out with good manners.
Reno is one of the smartest horses I've known.

He's tough and mentally strong. Instead of panicking at new
situations, Reno observes. He'll stand still with his head up, not
moving for the longest time while he surveys an area or watches
something I can't see. This kind of wild creature instinct kept his
ancestors alive. Rather than try to force him into a mold, my job
is to let him be who he is.

It's a big responsibility when a horse chooses a person as his
own.

His choice caused a few problems. At first, he had trouble sharing me with other people and bit at anyone who came near me.
While knowing my horse preferred me to everyone else might
flatter, I couldn't accept his behavior, and since he didn't want to
share me with people, he objected to other horses entering our personal space. If another horse approached me, Reno pinned his ears
and bared his teeth, ensuring the horse backed away. If I worked
with a different horse and then entered Reno's stall, my normally
friendly buddy would turn away as if to say, "I have other things
to do too." But Reno has mellowed and learned as he has grown.

We've developed a unique relationship. I gave in to his preferences in equipment. In the past, I used the closest brush for grooming. Through sniffing and his expression, Reno made it clear he disliked things that had another horse's scent. He wanted his own brushes.

If I wiggle a finger, Reno responds. He taught me to how to notice the little things—a huff, a twitch of his nostril, his eyelid fluttering. Time spent with Reno rejuvenated and healed me. Loyal, forgiving, smart, and honest, he has the qualities you look for in a best friend. His wild heritage makes him strong both in spirit and in body.

A dozen years have passed since our friendship began, and when I walk out my door, he pins his gaze on me. He looks forward to seeing me, whether I'm happy or need to lean into his broad back and cry. And I always look forward to seeing him. His presence lifts my spirits and helps me cherish the good things in my life. And by the way, he has the best manners of any horse on the farm, even around other people and horses.

People might think I saved a wild horse, but the truth is we saved each other.

17

With Harmony

Hope Ellis-Ashburn

A horse owner for nearly forty years, I thought I knew a thing or two about all things equine. In fact, not only have I owned horses for most of my life, but I have also studied them academically in college. If not an expert, I certainly considered myself well above average when it came to knowledge of their care and handling. But enter one determined donkey, and I soon realized how little I really knew.

Harmony's arrival on our farm brought the need for quick attention to farrier and veterinary care. Initially, Harmony's needs were paramount to everything else. However, the kind of handling required to get her immediate care was not something I wanted to do in the future. I longed for her to receive the sedative-free, pleasant handling that my horses were accustomed to receiving. The first step was for me to develop a friendship with an animal who had little desire to enjoy my company.

A small bag of treats and a large dose of patience brought about my first success. Spending time hanging out in Harmony's lot at a mutually agreed upon distance apart slowly began to bring her some measure of comfort with and curiosity about me. I offered treats from my outstretched hand but never forced myself on her.

Over a period of several days, she would greedily snatch a cookie from my hands and then quickly back away. I never gave chase, instead allowing her to decide when she felt comfortable enough to stand still and slowly chew her treat without feeling the need to disengage from my company.

Eventually, she allowed me to touch her muzzle and later her head and neck. As our relationship began to solidify, I thought about the best way to halter her without destroying our tenuous level of trust. I chose a thin cotton rope for the occasion, one that I could slip into the palm of my hand and hold as I stroked her. Slowly, she accepted the feel of the rope over her entire body. Even so, the first few times I tried quietly looping it loosely around her neck, she resumed her habit of quickly backing away.

I had recently learned some of the basics of positive reinforcement training, so I began using the treats for more than establishing a relationship. I began to use them to reward Harmony for exhibiting desired behaviors. In this manner, when she stood still and accepted the rope, I rewarded her with a treat.

While positive reinforcement training can be used with almost any animal, including horses and donkeys, what happened next, in spite of our successes, demonstrated that Harmony would continue to exert her independence in surprising ways.

My plan, once Harmony stood quietly with the rope looped around her neck, was to use the rope to accustom her to the feel of a halter. In other words, I would position the rope on areas of her head, such as behind her ears, under her throatlatch, or around her muzzle—areas where I hoped she would soon feel the slight pressure of a halter attached to a lead rope.

My success led to the purchase of a breakaway halter that I hoped would make her easier to catch in the pasture. But try as I might, the little donkey was adamant that her new green halter was not going over her head. After several days of failures and with a growing sense of frustration that we were moving backward rather than forward, I was forced to reconsider the situation. Was my new little donkey simply dimwitted or maybe even stubborn as donkeys are often portrayed to be? After all, I would have had the halter on most horses by now and be happily leading them about our farm. Harmony's bright and inquisitive nature eventually led me to rethink the situation.

After hanging her new halter back in the tack room, I came up with the idea to instead use a rope halter. Harmony immediately loved it. She clearly adored the lack of buckles and fasteners found on a traditional halter, preferring the soft, cottony feel of the type of rope to which she had become accustomed. The halter mystery solved, catching her, then leading for short distances at first and later for longer ones, progressed easily as long as I remembered to stop early and when it was my idea instead of hers.

Once able to catch and secure her, I began to focus on teaching her the skills necessary to receive good farrier and veterinary care. Relying on my newfound ability to listen, an old bag of training tricks, and positive reinforcement, I used a riding crop to gently tap and rub her legs. I rewarded her when she lifted them if only for a second at first. By listening to her body language, I started teaching the skill on the side where she felt most comfortable balancing, moving to the other only after she gained stability. As she progressed, I began to manipulate her hooves, much as my farrier would do, so that she felt less frightened by the experience.

Administering shots and dewormer were other concerns. But by now, I had learned that Harmony would freely tell me where she was most comfortable starting, and once we found that place, the teaching and learning could begin. At first, she wanted nothing to do with a syringe in her mouth. But when I filled empty dewormer syringes with applesauce and then wiped some on the outside of the tube, Harmony soon learned that the process of deworming could sometimes lead to a tasty treat. Next, allowing gentle pricks with toothpicks followed by a scrumptious treat led to the necessary acceptance of the needles used for vaccinations and sedatives, when needed, for the floating of her teeth. Over time, while Harmony was teaching me to be a better communicator, I was teaching her to be a better equid.

Today, years after I first brought her home, there is still work to be done. We are still perfecting our give-and-take communication skills to determine which brush she prefers for grooming. It's a chore that I hope one day becomes pleasurable for her. And, in spite of many attempts to acclimate her to other people, I am still her chosen person. Perhaps over time, she will learn to be as accepting of others as she is of me.

In the meantime, I am thankful for the many skills that Harmony has taught and continues to teach me. These skills play a major role in my communication with horses and other animals as well as with people. What I once deemed a reluctance to interact and learn was really a quiet yet firm and determined personality buried beneath layers of self-protection. Today Harmony demonstrates growing confidence that bubbles to the surface. I am forever grateful for the transformation and eager to see it continue to grow.

HOW IT STARTED

The Royal Society for the Prevention of Cruelty to Animals (RSPCA) started in England and Wales and was eventually endorsed by Queen Elizabeth II, who was, as we all know, a true lover of animals. When a similar society began in America—the ASPCA—it was formed initially to benefit horses. Of course, horses were crucial to everyday life in the nineteenth century, and yet they were subject to much unkindness. The ASPCA sought to change that. Their original logo shows a line drawing of a horse about to be struck by a man, but a large, determined angel is stepping between them. They've since expanded to offer help for all sorts of animals.

https://www.ASPCA.org/About-Us/History-Of-The-ASPCA

18

A Stable Trio

Glenda Ferguson

The Belgian pulling the carriage at the French Lick Resort was definitely noticeable. His chestnut coat gleamed, and his pale-yellow mane and tail looked as if they were groomed daily. That summer I was a volunteer being trained as a tour guide for this historical southern Indiana hotel. Often my tour group walked by the large horse, but I didn't want to get too close. I was only five feet in height, and this powerful equine was . . . well, taller. I certainly didn't know the Belgian's name, just his breed, or details about the other horses at the resort. I just assumed they had been purchased from an elite horse farm and lived a pampered life in a stable.

When my summer break was over, I returned to school for my last year as an elementary teacher. After forty-one years, I knew this was the time for me to retire. At last I would have more opportunities for accepting volunteer work and pursuing other passions.

The following summer, I noticed a different horse harnessed to the carriage. This one was a black Percheron with a white marking on his head. He clip-clopped by me on the brick roadway. When the driver stopped the carriage, the adults and children in my group were anxious to meet the black beauty. One of the smaller girls stretched up and scratched his nose. The others patted his glossy neck and rubbed on his back. They all seemed so relaxed around him. As for me, I grew up around pets like cats and kittens, dogs and puppies. It was not my natural tendency to be friendly toward horses.

I asked the driver what happened to the Belgian.

"That was Howdy. He's thirty-three years old now and he's retired," he said.

"Looks like Howdy and I retired at about the same time," I said. Then I commented on Howdy's easy life and speculated that he would be returned to a swanky farm.

"Oh no. This is his forever home. Besides, he didn't always have an easy life," he said. "Howdy used to be a logging horse and pulled heavy loads out of the woods. But he was very gentle."

I wasn't expecting to hear that.

The driver said, "Well, Jimmy here was a work horse too, and got used to doing hard labor. I've been working with him for a few weeks. He's made some mistakes, but I know he can do the job."

I was so wrong about both of these gentle giants. With Jimmy, this second chance included patience when mistakes were made. That gave me new insights about these horses. I realized if I made assumptions regarding their backgrounds, probably many others did too.

As a matter of fact, I suppose that was similar to the perceptions that other teachers had about me. They thought my education degree and my first teaching job came easily. Only a few of my closest friends knew my struggles. Despite my family's lack of finances, I earned my college tuition by waiting tables, washing dishes, and scrubbing dormitory floors.

My first teaching position came right out of college, but it ended five years later, when the school did away with my job. My next two teaching assignments were disasters. I could have given up on my dream of being a teacher, but I relied on the verse from Jeremiah 29:11: "'For I know the plans I have for you,' declares the LORD, 'plans to prosper you and not to harm you, plans to give you hope and a future.'" Regardless of previous setbacks, the fourth school hired me, and I stayed for the next thirty years.

As others were petting Jimmy, I summoned my courage. Stepping closer, I patted his sturdy side. Then I stroked his mane and touched his soft nose. I felt proud that I'd conquered some of my horse anxiety and gotten over my reluctance to know Jimmy.

Over the next few weeks, I settled into my retirement. Now was a perfect time to purse my passion for writing. I certainly wanted to make the attempt. But my fears about starting this second act surfaced. What if my writing was not accepted? How would I handle the rejection? With persistence, I finished a couple of stories and submitted them to an anthology. I waited and waited for the results. Admittedly, I was not patient; inside I fretted.

From time to time, while guiding a tour group, I heard the clip-clop of Jimmy's hooves and watched the carriage rolling along with passengers enjoying the excursion around the hotel grounds. Both Jimmy and I had completed our training so that we could perform a service for the hotel guests. When the carriage stopped, I greeted Jimmy, then approached him. I liked to think he was identifying my scent and my voice because his ears turned toward me. With the driver's urging, I decided to schedule a time to meet the other horses at the stables. He also suggested I go on a Friday so that I could have a photo with Pepsi. I wasn't sure what was so special about that horse and was a bit wary about posing with him.

One of the experienced trail riders gave me a guided tour of the stables. She said, "Before the horses are brought here, all of them are judged on their gentleness and calmness. Then they have to train for two years before we use them on trail rides with guests." She introduced me to many of the horses and ponies, goats and donkeys.

I asked my guide about meeting Pepsi. As we turned a corner, I saw a black and white, full-grown miniature horse. "Pepsi is very gentle. He's our stable mascot," she said.

Right away, I felt very comfortable approaching him, since he was . . . well, shorter than me.

"He's due for his summer haircut," the guide said.

I rubbed on his thick mane and shaggy back. Then I felt a scar running vertically down to his leg.

"Pepsi came from a situation where he needed to be rescued," my guide said. "Look at the white pattern on his side. I call them angel wings."

I was in awe of this diminutive horse. Pepsi remained calm while I petted him for several minutes. I promised the next time I visited I would bring him his favorite treat—bananas.

Perhaps my introduction to this trio of horses came along at just the right time. Reflecting on my visits, I realized I gained not only new insights about the horses' backgrounds but unexpectedly about myself. All along, I trusted in my teaching capabilities and persevered through the challenges. Looking toward the future, I was certain God would be guiding me with my writing career also. However, I needed to stress less and focus on remaining calm, like Pepsi did.

Still, there was so much to learn about the twenty-seven horses at the stable. I might even have the courage to request a trail ride. But I plan on taking it slow at first, by taking a ride in the carriage with Jimmy.

19

A Little Girl and Her Queen

Chris Kent

In a world full of princesses, I was always a cowgirl. While most little girls dreamed of dolls and dresses, I dreamed of horses. I collected statues of horses, and my bookshelf was filled with horse stories. A most cherished Christmas gift was *Misty of Chincoteague*. I spent hours astride an old army saddle on the railing of our porch, and the neighbors would wave and call out, "Hello, Dale Evans!" I waited impatiently for *My Friend Flicka* and *Black Beauty* to come to our local theater. I always dreamed that someday, one day, I would gallop across fields on my own horse.

On my eighth birthday, I blew out the candles on my cake, making the wish I made every year: *Please can I have a horse.* When I opened my eyes this time, I had no idea how my world was about to change. Indeed, my gift on my eighth birthday was a horse.

That first horse was a jumper named Red. He measured almost eighteen hands and was way too much horse for a little girl. My parents were not horse people and thought any horse would satisfy a little girl's dream. He came with a flat saddle and a bridle with two bits. I had to coax and cajole him to stand next to a gate so I could climb on and then hang on because he went where he wanted after that.

It soon became evident that a trade for a smaller, less spirited animal might be beneficial. The trade was made for the perfect little girl's horse—Queen. Before we met, quite probably Queen was destined for an unhappy end. She was an old saddle horse, limited by ring bone and living in a world of men who cared but scantily for a little girl's dreams. Her chances were running out.

An old stock truck braked on the road, engine rumbling. The vehicle turned and rattled down the drive of my grandparents' farm. With my pocket filled with sugar cubes, I awaited Queen's arrival.

"This here your horse?" the driver hollered at my grandfather as he climbed down out of the truck.

"I believe it is. Well, she belongs to this little girl." Grandpa tugged at my pigtail.

In my grandpa's life, horses were for work. All livestock was a commodity. The animals on the farm were well cared for, but they produced: horses worked, cows gave milk, pigs provided bacon, and chickens laid eggs. Now he stood beside me, welcoming a pet, a creature that would produce little except joy.

The driver, dressed in worn bib overalls, a plaid work shirt, and a battered brimmed felt hat, lowered the ramp and locked two side rails in place. He walked up the ramp. "Get over, you old fleabag," he muttered. I heard a loud slap, and then he led my horse down the steep ramp.

To me she was perfect—coal black and beautiful. My black beauty. The truck driver handed me the lead rope and without a word folded the ramp and drove off. Queen put her soft muzzle against my cheek, wiggling her lips to tickle my face. I pushed my hand into the pocket of my jeans and thrust a sugar cube out in my open hand. She nibbled the sweet treat.

In the months and years that followed, Queen and I would share endless miles and countless adventures. Queen would build my confidence, push my boundaries, and expand my skills and knowledge. I would care for her, love her, and ensure her safety.

Queen always loved the opportunity for a treat, an ice cream cone, an egg, or molasses drizzled on her grain. Gifts to reward her loyalty and trustworthiness. We once rode twenty miles in a blinding snowstorm to participate in the Maple Syrup Festival in a neighboring community. Upon arrival, we found a barn for shelter and ate pancakes dripping with syrup together. That was all she asked for her efforts.

Queen was not only dependable under saddle but became the community sweetheart by pulling a "surrey with the fringe on top" in every holiday parade. She wore ribbons in her mane and a carnation on either side of her bridle, and she held her head high as paradegoers along the route applauded. I'm sure she felt her stardom, her royalty.

Recently my brother passed away, and at the memorial, his friend since college shared a favorite Queen story. Sixty years earlier, this man's wife had been riding Queen when the horse stepped in a sinkhole created by a broken drain tile. Queen quickly sank to her belly. When I reached the scene, my heart was broken. I could not imagine a way to free the horse without injury or death. As I sank into the mire by her side, I stroked her head and neck in an attempt to calm her fears. Tears rolled off my cheeks and dripped into the muck as I clawed at the sludge around her legs. Eventually my brother and his friends joined me. Then a tractor arrived. With a sling around her mud-covered rump, we slowly aided Queen's own efforts to be free from the mire. Once on solid ground, my horse shook, mud flying, and nickered softly as I stroked her neck. Once again, Queen was rescued.

When I was twelve years old, my desire to become a cowgirl was finally realized. I was sitting in class, and a note arrived from the principal—I was to go to the office immediately. My classmates chided me as I gathered my books. "You're in trouble now."

But the reality was my grandpa's cattle had escaped their pen, and I was summoned to help round them up. I saddled Queen and headed across the field in pursuit of the fugitive steers. After chasing for what seemed like hours, it was not working like the cowboy shows. These steers ran in opposing directions with me in a desperate chase. Queen was getting tired, and I was discouraged, so we turned toward the farm to get more help. I looked over my shoulder to see the twelve steers fall in line behind me. We rode into the pen, followed by the steers, to a hero's welcome.

Some little girls outgrow their love for horses. Mine remained for a lifetime. Queen was my partner until one day, when I was in college, my dad came to see me and delivered the heartbreaking news that "Old Queen" had died. "She just didn't wake up one morning," Dad told me as he gave me a hug.

So much of who I am today grew from those days with my horse at my grandparents' farm. I may have been her second chance, but she was my dream.

Ivan, My Teacher

Karen Thurman

Most of us have heard the adage "Life is what happens while you're busy making other plans." When I hear that, I always smile and nod, knowing how true it is. As I grow long in the tooth and look back, I cannot imagine my life any different than it is today. But my life now is not what I imagined at all.

I was that young girl who was born loving horses. Everything about them made my little heart skip a beat when I was around them. Their big fluid eyes, their velvety muzzles, their sounds and smells. Someday, I told myself, I would have my own horse. I thought of wonderful names for them. I envisioned what color my horse would be and how he would carry me gently across open pastures. We'd be best friends and share our most intimate secrets.

I worked hard while growing up and got a job as soon as someone would hire me. I saved my money and bought a farm and then sold it and bought a bigger one. And yes, I had horses along the way. My second farm was an amazing 185 acres of grass and trees. I had a big barn built and a riding ring where I taught horsemanship. I loved every horse that I touched. Each one was special. I can still see their beautiful faces and hear their soft nickers when they saw me. I took in boarders and continued teaching during the day as I still worked at night to help pay the bills.

The months and years passed quickly. Somewhere along the way I quit teaching horsemanship and began resting Standardbred racehorses when they needed a soft place to land. I loved helping these tired and sometimes injured warriors off the track. It was always rewarding to see the spark of happiness return to their beautiful eyes.

When the owner of the Standardbreds decided to "get out of racing" and sent all of his horses to an auction, I was suddenly almost horseless. I still had my own thirteen school horses, but the almost fifty racehorses were gone. I took a deep breath and decided to take a little time to figure out what I really wanted to do next.

Selling my farm was not an option. Helping horses was my true passion. I wanted to be the answer, the reason, and the hope for the horses who had given up on us humans. At the time, it all seemed so simple. I would rescue horses! I could go to auctions and buy the saddest, thinnest horses and make their lives wonderful. My mind's eye could see them grazing in lush pastures as the gentle breezes tossed their manes about. It would be a great life for all of us with enough happiness for everyone. Yes, I had a plan and could not wait to get started.

But this is where life steps in wearing big boots. Out of nowhere, I got a call from someone seeking a home for a blind horse. A blind horse? I didn't know anything about blind horses. So it's a horse who can't see. How hard can this be? (Famous last words.)

I said I'd take him. And if you think I'm going to say, "And the rest is history," you're right. But history was not made in one day, and neither was the complicated system of caring for blind horses.

The blind horse in question, I was told, was a buggy horse from a local Amish family. A Standardbred, no doubt, probably older, maybe broken down from years of pounding on hard surfaces. And blind to boot.

Soon the horse arrived. The older bay gelding was sound and very willing as he was led off the trailer. He seemed curious, not frightened, and a bit relieved, I'm sure, as he was gently taken to a clean stall I had prepared for him. I was told by the hauler that the horse had worked that morning pulling his owners on their daily rounds. The lady of the Amish family was the nurse and midwife of their community, and this blind horse had been her trusted transportation for years. The big bay was strong, and I'm sure if not for his blindness, he could have worked many more years for his Amish family.

That year, Hurricane Ivan was roaring through Florida and points south. Ah, the perfect name for my horse. I christen thee: Ivan. And Ivan it was for almost fifteen years.

Let me go back now to day two.

The morning after his arrival, Ivan ate his breakfast with great gusto. I put him out in a side paddock close to the barn where I could keep a good eye on him. Oddly, every time I glanced around the corner, he was standing by the gate, waiting. To come in? No—probably to go to work. Old habits die hard, they say, and Ivan was a worker. Retirement was not on his radar.

Poor guy. That was the hardest thing for Ivan to understand. For me, the hardest thing was remembering that each horse is different, even in their blindness. They all want and need different things.

And so my education began. Ivan was the perfect teacher as he never overreacted to me. His years of being a blind buggy horse taught him well, and his former owners did him a real favor by continuing to use him even as his world grew dark. Ivan finally accepted his retirement and appeared happy in his new job as teacher to the "lady who wants to rescue blind horses"—me.

I learned that sightless horses listen very carefully. I discovered that tapping on Ivan's food buckets let him know where his food was. The tapping worked a lot like clicker training, and he responded to the sound even out in the field when I needed him to come inside. Ivan got along with all the other horses, but sometimes there would be a bully, and a sightless horse is an easy target. Seeing a blind horse being picked on is scary. I learned early on not to mix blind with sighted; even the most well-adjusted horse can panic when being bullied.

After a suitable amount of time, Ivan was given a BFF—that's a blind, furry friend. Ivan fell in love with Coco, who was also blind, and she became his constant companion. He watched over his sweetheart with all the care in the world.

Ivan passed away at thirty-four, quietly, in his stall. For me, it was like a slap, hard and loud, and then silent tears. He was never angry about his blindness. He persevered and finished the race a winner. He taught me that life is not what we see but what we feel. His quiet acceptance of his fate and his happiness at a life still worth living was an inspiration.

And beyond that, Ivan showed me I could care for blind horses and give them a good life. Thanks to his intelligence and patience, I now have thirty-nine blind horses to love. I have learned a lifetime of knowledge and understanding from these remarkable horses. They have so much to share and teach to anyone who will stop, look, and listen.

Open your heart and feel, Ivan taught me. Life is what we make it.

The Horses of Graceland

Deborah Camp

Almost everyone raised in Memphis, Tennessee, during the fifties and sixties—as I was—has an Elvis story. One of my friends sold Girl Scout cookies to him when he opened the door at Graceland one afternoon. Another friend met him when the interior design company she worked for upholstered some sofas in his living room. I have my own memory of meeting Elvis I've enjoyed and carried with me all my life—a memory that influenced much of my later work with animal rescue.

My mom was a huge Elvis fan. I remember us jitterbugging in the living room while Dad was at work. We slid around the hardwood floor in white cotton bobby socks as a lavender plastic transistor radio blasted out the sounds of "Don't Be Cruel" and "Jailhouse Rock."

One hot Sunday afternoon when I was ten, Dad, who was not particularly fond of Elvis but was fond of minimizing my mother's nagging, drove our family and my best friend Peggy Jo out to Highway 51 in the direction of Graceland. Mom wanted to see if by chance Elvis might be out in his front yard.

He was! The wide iron gates adorned with musical notes were open, and we could see Elvis! He was sitting atop a beautiful brown horse on the grassy front lawn of the stately colonial-style mansion, laughing and signing autographs for a gaggle of young women. "Oh, my *goodness*, he's really *here*!" Mom whispered.

Dad cautiously drove his blue Chevrolet halfway up the driveway. Mom rummaged through her pocketbook and thrust a fountain pen and blank postcard into my hands. With firm instructions to get an autograph, Peggy Jo and I scrambled from the car and raced up the driveway toward Elvis on his horse, while my parents, younger sister, and brother watched from the car.

Teenage girls elbowed and pushed their way closer to their idol. Peggy Jo and I wriggled our skinny ten-year-old selves to the front of the throng until I was right in front of the horse and eye-to-eye with Elvis's black riding boots. I felt the heat radiating from his magnificent horse and could smell its earthy odor. Elvis stroked the big animal's head, touched his ears, and swatted flies from his face.

Suddenly I heard the panicked voice of Peggy Jo. "Help! His horse is stepping on my foot!" she shrieked. I looked down, and sure enough, Elvis's otherwise gentle horse was resting his gigantic hoof on top of Peggy Jo's white Keds sneakers.

Normally I was a polite and shy sort of kid, but my friend was in trouble and bold measures were required. I reached my spindly arms as high as I could and yanked Elvis's pants leg. When that didn't get his immediate attention, I swatted at him as hard as I could.

Elvis looked down at me with that famous smile and cerulean eyes and asked, "What's the matter, little lady?"

My face turned crimson. "Get your horse off my friend's foot!"

Elvis gently raised the reins, and his horse eased back. "Sorry 'bout that, little lady!"

The crowd parted, and we sprinted back to the car. We spilled into the back seat, breathlessly relating our disastrous encounter. Mom stared at my empty hands and looked like she was going to cry. The only thing she was interested in was his autograph.

Dad laughed. "Ah, come on, Dot. That boy ain't ever gonna be *that* famous."

Dad's lack of foresight aside, that day was a life-changing experience for me. Seeing my preteen idol exhibiting such a connection with his horse cemented my interest in animals and rescue. Seventeen years later, at the moment I learned of Elvis's passing, my thoughts flashed on that day at Graceland. I conjured the image of Elvis on his horse and how he looked down and smiled at me with the most beautiful blue eyes I'd ever seen. I particularly remembered how lovingly he treated his horse.

Over the years I became involved with animal welfare and rescue in Memphis. One year I created a fundraiser for the local Humane Society called "Don't Be Cruel . . . to Animals." Graceland issued licensing rights to use Elvis's image on T-shirts and gave their enthusiastic support for what became one of the most successful fundraisers the nonprofit had ever sponsored.

As I got to know fans who participated in the nonprofit event, I realized that many Elvis fans were very devoted to their pets. I came to believe there was a strong association between Elvis—a true animal lover—and fans who felt that same loyalty to their own animals. It also seemed to me like the devotion and affection I saw Elvis express with his horse was similar to the devotion and affection he had for his fans. It was as if an emotional current flowed through him and his music and connected to the joy that could be found in loving an animal. In fact, a couple of his most popular and celebrated songs had animal themes—"Hound Dog" and "Old Shep."

I discovered dusty old scrapbooks in the office of the Humane Society containing copies of original letters revealing Elvis's longtime financial support of the organization. But in no area of animal welfare was Elvis more dedicated than to the horses in his care.

Through my rescue involvement, I had the opportunity to talk to Priscilla Presley on the phone. This was a thrill for me, and I felt as if I were chatting with an old girlfriend. I learned that in their marriage, she and Elvis enjoyed many pets and spared no expense for their care. But once Elvis fell in love with horses, he was smitten. Graceland would eventually become a haven for some fortunate horses in need of second chances.

It began when Elvis presented Priscilla with a Christmas gift in their early years together. "I had no idea what he was up to," Priscilla recalled. "He'd been gone for a while, but later that day he said, 'Come outside, I've got something for you.'"

Outside stood a handsome, black, four-year-old quarter horse named Domino. "I instantly loved him," Priscilla said. "We bonded from the start, and soon I was riding him every day while Elvis watched from the window."

It didn't take long for Elvis to see how much joy Domino brought Priscilla. He began searching for a horse he could ride alongside her, and perhaps even with his friends. As he immersed himself in his newfound interest, Elvis began fixing up the original stables at Graceland. He named the stables House of the Rising Sun, in honor of the golden palomino he bought for himself named Rising Sun.

Elvis acquired trucks, trailers, riding clothes, and all sorts of equestrian equipment to support his growing passion. He found solace in his land and in his horses. "He was personally involved with everything that went on in the stable," Priscilla recalled. "He wanted to tack and harness each horse. And he wanted everyone in his circle—from his friends to his bodyguards—to have a horse." She laughed. "It didn't matter if you didn't want a horse, you were going to *get* a horse!"

Riding horses together on the thirteen-acre estate was among the most rewarding and joyful times of Priscilla's life, she recalled. "It was the horses that made Graceland home to us." Elvis never seemed happier than when they rode together or when he was organizing the stable. Sometimes in the wee hours of the morning, he would work in the stables and paint the stalls. Taking care of the horses and stables was a good outlet for him and helped him relax from the stresses of fame.

Over the years, many horses came to live at Graceland. Among them were Memphis, a bay Tennessee Walking Horse, and Mare Ingram—a horse named in honor of Memphis Mayor Ingram, who was responsible for renaming Highway 51 Elvis Presley Boulevard. There was Bear, who was Elvis's beloved Tennessee Walking

Horse, and many others. Ebony's Double was the last horse Elvis purchased for Graceland in 1975.

On August 16, 1977, the world reverberated with the news of Elvis Presley's death. Fans from across the country—as if drawn by some invisible magnet—assembled outside the gates of Graceland to unite in their collective grief. I always figured the horses also felt this tremendous loss.

After Elvis's passing, Graceland became a refuge for a handful of lucky horses in need of second chances. Although the stables were never designed to be a rescue facility, Priscilla intended to keep alive the spirit of Elvis's compassion and generosity by offering a helping hand to horses when she could.

In 2008, days after what would have been Elvis's 73rd birthday, Priscilla adopted Max, a horse scheduled for slaughter. She found out about him from a fundraiser that was created when his owner could no longer afford him. At one point, celebrities signed T-shirts for an auction for Max. Those celebrities included country music artist Alan Jackson, *Extreme Makeover: Home Edition* host Ty Pennington, former Catwoman actress Julie Newmar, and other well-known animal lovers.

Priscilla was also on the celebrity list. By then she had become a vocal advocate for animals in trouble. This time, she went a step further and adopted Max. She decided he could live out his life at Graceland. Her beloved horse lived a comfortable eleven years before passing away in 2019.

Second chances were offered again in an animal cruelty case in a nearby county. Neighbors reported animals being mistreated on a farm, and cruelty investigators found horses on the brink of death. When Priscilla learned about the case, she offered to take in one of the rescues named Bandit. At that time, Bandit was still young, skinny, and traumatized. But today, Bandit is sixteen years old—thriving and happy at Graceland.

Tucker was a horse who lived in a herd that included his mother. That mare died when Tucker was nine years old, and the young horse sank into depression. When a series of circumstances unfolded that required Tucker to find a new home, he was offered a forever home at Graceland. He lives there today, enjoying his life at age twenty-six.

Priscilla has been happy offering a haven for the rescues she's adopted over the years. "Our stable is not that big," she told me. "We only have limited stalls and they're full. But I'm doing what I can to get the message out on the importance of rescue."

These days, visitors to Graceland can view the stables as part of their tour. Since horses were such a happy part of Elvis's life, having them roam Graceland—living their good lives—was important to Priscilla. She continues to cherish the memories of when she and Elvis rode their horses together on the grounds of Graceland every day.

As for me, whenever I drive by Graceland or attend an event there, I'm taken back to that day I met Elvis on his horse. I became a lifelong Elvis fan and an animal lover—particularly a lover of horses. I was further inspired to work in rescue by Priscilla.

That Graceland became a safe harbor for horses as well as the home for numerous other adopted pets is usually one of the first things I tell visiting friends who want to hear about Elvis's Graceland from a native Memphian. I like to tell them I see Graceland from three perspectives. First, it's the home where Elvis lived as the world's most famous rock 'n' roller. Second, it's the mansion Priscilla transformed into the second-most-visited home museum in the United States.

And third, I see Graceland as a place imbued with the spirit of Elvis and his horses. Although his music will forever perpetuate his legacy as a performer and musician, horses will always preserve the image of the person Elvis really was. And with the rescue horses on view to visitors, anyone who makes the pilgrimage to Graceland will carry away a little of that spirit with them.

I do every time.

22

Miracle in the Barn

Kristi Ross

"Record low temperatures," the TV newsman blared out. I pulled on my boots and grabbed another jacket. Foxy wasn't due for another month, but with the barometric pressure crash, I feared she might foal early. I knew that animals are just as sensitive to the barometric pressure as humans are. It can aggravate arthritis and even cause a baby to come too early.

I gathered my gloves, headlamp, flashlight, and truck keys. Then I took a deep breath and opened the door. A blast of arctic air pummeled me. Howling wind whipped the Colorado snow with blinding force. I put my head down and marched into the wind.

All the mares were in the barn, but, just as I feared, Foxy was off by herself at the back. Something was wrong. I grabbed a halter and a bucket of grain and dropped small handfuls in each feed tub to keep the other mares away from Foxy. When I saw the small, seemingly lifeless body lying in the dirt, my heart leaped to my throat. Everything in me feared that I was too late. The little guy was a mass of blood and matted manure. It was a hideous sight.

I rushed to Foxy's side and haltered her. Then I knelt to see if there was any hope for the tiny foal. He was damp and cold—too cold. But he had a heartbeat and was breathing. Barely.

I pulled off my outer jacket and wrapped the newborn foal in it. I wouldn't be wearing this jacket again, but it would be worth the loss if I could save the little guy. I picked him up. Being a month early, he was far lighter than he should have been. I rushed toward the gate and threw it open.

Foxy followed behind, softly nickering to her near lifeless baby. My heart went out to her as I carried her little one to a nearby foaling stall I had prepared for a different mare. I gently laid him on the fresh pine shavings. The clean scent of pine gave me hope. Foxy stood over him as I tried to figure out how to rub the foal dry and get him warm. I needed towels. While rubbing the foal with one hand, I dug into my coat pocket for my phone with the other, praying for enough service to call out.

Thankfully the phone rang, and I heard John say hello. John was the neighbor boy who came and helped me around the place and fed the horses for me when I went out of town. He was sixteen, big and strong, and would do anything to help me.

"I'm at the barn," I said. "Can you please grab as many rags as you can and come help me with a foal?"

"Did you say bring rags?"

"Yes, please. And hurry!"

"I'll be right there."

I had the foal as clean as my jacket would get him, but he was still soaking wet and needed more help. Five minutes later, John's headlights flickered across the barn walls. He ran toward me with an armload of rags and towels and dropped them at my feet. "Dad said to call if we need him, and Mom said not to worry about the towels. They're old."

I picked up a rag and started rubbing. "We need to save this little guy. He's terribly cold, and he's a month too early. But I think we can get him warm enough."

John and I worked, feverishly rubbing the little foal, but his mouth was still ice-cold, which is a terrible sign. I didn't mention that fact to John because with every wipe of the towel, the teenager drew closer and closer to the foal. He was quickly invested in what he was doing. I heard him speaking tender words to the little one, and I felt in my heart that John was growing attached to him.

When the foal was finally dry, John and I were both exhausted. We sat silent in the fluffy shavings with the foal's head in my lap and his hips and hind legs in John's. John's hands caressed the little foal as if he could rub life back into him. I wanted so much for this little foal to live, but his closed eyes were not moving. The only sounds were the tiny tinkling of snow hitting the tin roof and the occasional shuffle of the other horses.

My hand was on the foal's ribs. They were still, too still, and there was no heartbeat. I didn't say anything to John, but the tears in his eyes told me he already knew. It was too late. It looked like there would be no chance for the little guy.

I broke the silence. "Let's pray for him."

John looked up. "Seriously? For a horse?"

I nodded. "It says in the Bible that not a sparrow falls that the Lord does not see. So yes, for a horse."

He shrugged. "Ooookay."

We bowed our heads and I said, "Dear Father in heaven, you and I both know this little foal is not gonna make it without your touch. You say that not a sparrow falls that you don't see. So we ask that you heal this little foal."

Nothing. Still no breath.

I looked back at John. "Would you like to pray for him?"

He shook his head. "I'm not very good at praying."

"Just say what you feel in your heart."

John looked uncertain, but he began, "Dear Jesus, please save this baby horse. Amen."

As soon as John said, "Amen," the foal took several deep gasps. John's eyes grew large. He looked at me and whispered, "Did you see that?"

I wasn't sure what I saw. Perhaps these were death sounds. But the foal gasped again. I stuck my finger in his mouth and felt warmth come back. A moment later the foal opened his eyes and nickered.

Foxy stepped forward and nuzzled her baby. In a few minutes the little foal was trying to get up. We helped him, and then guided him to his momma's milk. Thirty minutes later, our little miracle stood there on wobbly legs, looking at us all through big, bright, totally healthy eyes.

John and I walked out of the barn, both of us very grateful. A little foal lived. And John had learned how to pray!

23

Mystique

Catherine Ulrich Brakefield

"She's too good a horse to be treated this way," the trainer said.

My daughter reached over and stroked the dirty coat of the mare. "You need a bath, don't you, girl?" Kimberly loved animals—horses in particular, especially mistreated and abused horses. It was as if her purpose in life was to nurse every wounded bunny, abused cat, or mistreated puppy. Animals were more soulmates to her than her schoolmates were.

Earlier that day, my husband and I hoped a nice drive in the country might loosen the lips of our teenager. That she'd confide in us regarding the new friends she made this freshman year at Oxford High. One parent during registration whispered that many of the kids attending Oxford High School thought bullying classmates was a fun pastime. Kim hadn't mentioned any ill behavior.

But only silence emerged from the back seat.

The older my daughter became, the less she wanted to say. Was this the norm for a teenager these days? We felt like something was wrong. But asking, demanding, or probing never worked.

"We should be at the horse farm soon," I said.

Kim remained mummified.

She never was the outgoing type. Still, I didn't remember her ever being this quiet. She'd attended Christian schools until now, and though she didn't talk much about it, I knew the transition into a public high school must be challenging. Kim, however, had been excited to go—so what happened?

Then one afternoon she jumped off the bus and ran up the driveway. "Mom, Oxford High's equestrian team needs a saddle seat rider. I can do this." The sudden smile on her face, the bounce in her step—I jumped at the challenge of finding the perfect horse for her in hopes this would make her four years in high school easier to endure.

Now, as we drove down a blacktopped road, the scenery changed. A horse farm came into view. The spacious arena and barns sat majestically on a grassy hillside. White fences bordered a broad curving driveway. I felt confident our search may be over.

Edward, my husband, slowed down as the driveway came into view. To the left of a dirt drive stood about ten or more horses, some with protruding bellies, heavy in foal. Their paddock was nothing but mud. The horses' legs and underbellies were caked with it. Their matted manes and tails gave witness to their ill-kept condition, that they hadn't been groomed for months if not years.

One flea-bitten gray mare captured my attention. Her large black eyes looked into mine for a split second. I muttered, "Girl, if I could rescue you, I would."

We entered the stable's office. The owner of the establishment told a girl who looked to be around twelve to get Mystique. After a short while, amazement rippled through my body when the horse I had seen in the muddy paddock walked before us, being ridden bareback with only a halter by the young girl. Kim and I followed them to the grooming stall. My husband, Edward, followed the owner toward the arena.

Kim was a good cross-country equestrian, mostly due to the foxhunting club we rode in. But the Oxford equestrian team was full up on hunt seat riders. Kim needed to do saddle seat. That's where they needed her. I had to find a horse who knew her stuff, so to speak, to help with this dilemma. Kim's fingers tapped nervously on the half-wooden railing of the stall.

I patted my daughter on the shoulder and said to the trainer grooming this mare, "I don't understand. Are you sure you don't have the wrong horse? This is the show horse the owner sold for ten thousand dollars four years ago?"

"Yes." The trainer nodded. "The owner entered Mystique when she was three years old into the state finals. Mystique won the saddle seat competition and at the Michigan Arabian Horse Show. A man bought her the next day. Then the bottom fell out of Michigan's auto plants, and the purchaser pleaded with my boss to take her back." He shrugged. "The owner gave the man back his money and decided to breed Mystique. She's had three foals since then."

Mystique lowered her head. Her mane was so tangled and matted I wondered at the trainer's patience in untangling the matted mess. "Why doesn't the owner take better care of her broodmares? The stallions have a comfy stall."

"That's the way things are in most barns what with the present economy." He patted her affectionally. "Four years ago, she had a big stall, was groomed every day. You should have seen her in her show days, all shiny. Her mane was silky to the touch and her coat glistened with vitality."

"Right," Kim said. "Four years can seem like an eternity if you do nothing meaningful—no one even knowing you exist." I watched as she hung her head and walked into the arena. I glanced back at Mystique before leaving the grooming stall. I couldn't imagine this horse ever well-kept, admired, or needed for her performance skills.

I had shown saddle seat a few times. I preferred riding the wide-open spaces to going around and around in a show ring. I was as green as a grasshopper on how to prepare my daughter for her new venue. As I walked into the arena, my conscience reminded me that I promised to rescue this horse if there was any way possible.

Could Mystique possibly be the right horse for my daughter? The horse was a has-been. Probably didn't even have enough energy to canter, let alone gallop. And there was no way my husband would pay anything close to what Mystique's owner wanted—not now.

The owner smiled pleasantly at me. She was a petite blond, with a fair complexion and large blue eyes. "The trainer will tack Mystique up," she said. "Probably put on the harness first. She hasn't had a saddle on her back for a while."

"My daughter's a good rider," Edward said. "She's got a nice cross-country gelding, Baja, but he doesn't like arenas. We were looking for a trained saddle seat horse at a reasonable price. I don't see—"

"Mystique is a proven show horse," the owner interrupted.

The trainer walked out with Mystique saddled and wearing a training harness. He pulled the apparatus tighter, forcing Mystique to arch her neck in a dramatic pose. Then he took the lunging whip and, with the draw reins attached to the training harness, lunged her in circles.

Edward crossed his arms over his chest and shrugged. "I never saw a horse arch its neck so dramatically like that before. Does it hurt her?"

"Not in the least," the owner said. "She's used to this. The trainer is getting her to the spot she was before we used her for a broodmare."

Mystique didn't complain. She obeyed every command and displayed a willing disposition. The temperament of a horse is the most important asset to me. I glanced at my daughter, who appeared excited yet somewhat apprehensive. She probably felt a little out of her league, as did we all.

"Okay, who wants to ride her first?" the owner said.

"I will." I placed my foot into the iron and swung into the saddle, then gathered the reins. She was a little shorter than my mare. The trainer showed me the way to handle the draw reins. I had two reins in each hand. I coaxed her forward. Mystique's head was bowed so drastically I asked the trainer, "Am I holding the reins too tightly?"

"Nope, they're fine."

Well, the first thing that would go were those fancy draw reins. Mystique had the springiest trot I ever rode. I sure missed my comfy hunt saddle with my nice knee rolls. I put her back to a walk and then gave her the canter cue. She went into that smoothly. The mare knew her gaits well.

"Mom?" Kimberly stepped forward. Eagerness swelled like sunshine through her jubilant grin. Was it only for the horse or was it partly due to a newfound hope—being appreciated and needed by students and faculty?

Kimberly mounted Mystique and picked up the reins like a trooper. Obeying every command, Mystique assuredly noticed this was a young stranger on her back. My daughter maneuvered her legs and seat in the unaccustomed style of the flat seat saddle much better than I had. I chuckled. Kim's seat improved with every stride of Mystique's bouncy trot. They appeared to understand each other. Coming around the third time, they had become one fluid pair. A kinship had blossomed before my eyes in that split second, and somehow I knew in my heart it would endure.

"Kim's going to need some saddle seat lessons on Mystique," my husband commented.

The owner nodded. "Yes, I include three lessons with every purchase of one of my horses."

"Well, we need to negotiate on the price."

I prayed. My husband loved to bicker prices, but I had a hunch the owner wasn't so keen about that.

The owner chuckled. "Your daughter is a good rider, and I can tell that Mystique likes her. I can go lower on the price. Would you like me to throw in a breeding to sweeten the sale?"

Edward had looked the stallions over while Kim and I were with Mystique. "What do you say, Cathy, you want Mystique?"

Mystique's ears pricked forward, her eyes alert and focused, as were my daughter's—on me. They deserved this chance. And I'd be keeping my word.

I stroked Mystique's head and murmured, "You can rescue each other."

Kimberly leaned over and hugged Mystique's neck. She swung down off the saddle and gave Mystique another hug. "We've got a chance, girl."

24

Third Time's a Charm

Connie Webster

I was in way over my head. I had retired my laminitic older trail horse and was looking for a suitable replacement. I had brought home a beautiful black Percheron filly named Beauty who had been rescued by a friend from a bad situation. The plan was to give her the safe home she deserved and to train her to be my solid trail buddy.

Unfortunately, the filly had almost no handling and had nothing but mistrust and contempt for humans. I'd had horses for many years, but I'd never been around one who had been so mishandled as to be quite dangerous. Though she would appear passive and gentle at times, she would suddenly and without warning explode and begin bucking and rearing. More than once, she headed toward me full speed with the intent to intimidate me and remove me from her pasture. In spite of all this, I felt pity for the young horse who had been mishandled and ill-treated. I kept trying to overcome my fears and continued to attempt to work with her.

One day after a particularly explosive encounter with Beauty, I realized I could not keep her any longer and hope to train her. I had too much fear of her, and she knew it, as horses do. I contacted a trainer who had tried to help me with her. He was able to place her with a seasoned trainer who, after working with her extensively, was so impressed with her abilities that he wanted to use her as his posse horse. I thought that was a perfect fit for her personality. She had performed well for him, and for that I was happy. I was glad to help Beauty find her perfect niche, even it if meant she moved on. But now I was back to square one as far as finding a dependable trail mount.

Enter my Rocky. He was eight years old. A gaited Morgan gelding the color of creamy hot cocoa with a flaxen mane and tail, he was not only beautiful, but he was also a reliable and trustworthy trail horse. He proved himself many times to be everything a trail horse could and should be. He was steady on the trails and gentle with my grandchildren. He loaded into my trailer with never an issue. He watched out for me and was perhaps the kindest horse I have ever had. Sadly, he had a condition called heaves (COPD), which continued to grow worse each year in spite of all my attempts to treat his condition. Eventually for his own comfort and peace, I laid him to rest. I was devastated.

But God opened another door for me, and a spunky red roan trotted right through it and into my life. My husband had seen my sadness at the loss of my dear Rocky. He encouraged me to begin looking for a good trail horse, so I took him seriously and did some horse shopping. He likes to joke that one day he said I needed to find another horse, and a week later there was a new horse in the pasture. It truly happened that fast.

The fact was that Roanie (not a very creative name, but it fit him well) had been passed from one owner to another in short succession and was on the market yet again. When I found him, he was in need of some good care and a few hundred pounds.

At our first meeting, Roanie was being kept at a boarding facility until he could be sold. We are all aware that first impressions are lasting ones and often set the tenor of that relationship. At our initial meeting, I walked out into a large pasture with multiple horses gathered around a large round bale. Roanie ambled up to me and moved his face near mine, and with quiet eyes, he sighed a slow breath that spoke to me of relief. We placed a halter on him, and he led out quietly and nicely. So far so good.

Roanie was curious as we saddled him with an old, stiff saddle that they had lying around. We then rummaged around for a barely suitable bit and bridle for him. When I mounted him, he stood quietly and turned his head to me in his curious way. There was a main road right next to the arena, and as it was late afternoon, trucks and general heavy traffic moved noisily past us as we took our initial ride. Roanie was attentive and showed himself to be willing to listen to yet another unknown human asking him to perform. It took just that one ride for me to determine that he was the right one for me and that I was looking at my new partner.

Once I had my new horse home, he settled in nicely. But I was unsure of his abilities as a dependable trail horse, so Roan and I rode to my friend's farm. It was our first outing, and my friend Merry was riding a horse who was new to her. As we headed out and turned a corner, we were surprised by two noisy cranes stalking across the road closely ahead of us. They passed in and out among the tall weeds, causing them to sway back and forth. As with many riding situations, there was no time to think or prepare for it. Roanie just stopped and looked at the cranes for a few seconds, then he continued down the road as if it were nothing unusual. His response helped my friend's horse to move on as well. Roanie passed his first test with flying colors.

Since then, we have trailered several times to ride with friends. We have ridden through woods and streams and up switchbacks and along some rough terrain. He has proven himself to be exactly the right horse for me. He's spunky with a bit of attitude, which is just what I need. His slight impatience keeps me on my toes as we move along.

My Roanie is now twelve and full of zip and personality. He is always ready for scratches and bits of apple or carrot that he asks for in his funny way. He makes me laugh every day with his silly antics. Then he gently places his beautiful head in my arms for warm hugs. We have been together for three years now, and our bond continues to grow. I'm not sure who rescued whom, but either way I'm very thankful for my spunky boy. I hope to continue to ride him into our sunset years.

25

Rodeo's Princess

Katherine Pasour

Leaves on towering oaks shading the pasture barely stirred in a weak summer breeze as I finished the morning chores. The sun, not long over the horizon, promised another hot, sultry day. A persistent horsefly buzzed me as I propped a foot on the gate and rested elbows on the top plank. Spying some available skin, the horsefly thought to take a bite of my forearm, but a quick slap ended his plan. A seemingly endless supply of the bloodthirsty insects buzzed around my head and pestered the single occupant of the pasture.

The despondent horse kept his tail in constant motion as he turned a baleful eye toward me. Noticing the absence of a feed bucket in my hands, he again lowered his head and sighed. I crawled through the railings of the gate to approach him. He grunted as I scratched behind his ears, turning his head in an attempt to rub against me.

"Oh no you don't, big boy." I blocked his move to scrub his face against my shoulder. "That's one bad habit we haven't been able to break you of in all these years, and I guess it's too late now." I rubbed the side of his face to appease him and gently eased his head to forward position again. Giving his ears another good scratching, I earned another satisfied grunt.

"Rodeo, you miss your buddy, don't you?" I ran my fingers through his mane as memories surrounded me. His pasture mate had died the previous year, and the old sorrel gelding felt the absence of his friend deeply. "I miss him too," I murmured, probably more to comfort myself than the stocky quarter horse who again ignored me. Without an offer of food, he wasn't interested in conversation, and a check of my pockets found no horse treats.

We'd owned his absent pasture mate, Go-Boy, a feisty Arabian, for many years. Although I'd had a horse as a child, Go-Boy was my first horse as an adult. He lived up to his name—he liked to go. A spirited horse suited me just fine since I liked to go too. As he'd aged, Go-Boy settled down, and we grew older and slower together.

As my daughter became old enough to ride with me, we needed another horse. My husband inquired among his acquaintances, and we found a neighbor anxious to sell. I rode this newly purchased addition to our family more than five miles on the shoulders of rural roads to bring him to our farm. Every step of the way, the stubborn equine fought to turn around and go home. Only the fact that his rider was even more stubborn brought about our arrival to the farm.

Our new addition came to us named Rattlesnake. We hadn't inquired as to the history of the name but hoped it wasn't an omen of hard times ahead with our new horse.

We decided to start with a clean slate and renamed him Rodeo. Later, he would live up to his new name as he tested us in numerous ways and exuberantly bucked me off during a trail ride and raced home without me. But for the most part, Rodeo settled in, although his stubborn streak never disappeared.

Rodeo and Go-Boy immediately bonded. They skirmished and picked on each other like two middle school boys but loved one another as brothers. Like people, horses are social animals—they don't like to be alone.

Now, after years with Go-Boy as a companion, Rodeo lived in solitude, alone and sad. He was older and we no longer rode him, but he wasn't adjusting to the absence of his friend. We didn't know how to help him get over his sorrow.

But then . . .

My husband, a social and friendly man, seemed to know everyone and all the news in our community. Another neighbor was in possession of an abandoned horse. Someone had asked him to keep the horse for a short time, and he never saw the owner again. He wanted the horse out of his pasture. When we visited to check out the horse in need of rescue, we found a little white Arabian mare, thin, skittish, and afraid of her own shadow.

Our teenage daughter was immediately smitten with the timid horse, and we decided to take her. She came without a name, and our daughter christened her Princess Leia.

We brought our little girl home, unloaded her, and placed her in a pasture adjacent to Rodeo. The old horse's head shot up as he stared at the new arrival. He shouted a welcome with a hearty snort. Head high and tail plumed in show-off mode, he pranced back and forth across his pasture, trumpeting his excitement with constant neighs of, "Look at me, you lovely little horse!"

He came close to the pasture fence separating him from this new and fascinating creature and preened some more as if to say, "I like you, you pretty thing. What do you think of me?"

Being shy, Princess Leia remained aloof and didn't get within touching range. But that didn't stop Rodeo from hanging over the fence, fascinated by this vision of loveliness who had suddenly appeared in his life. The old horse became a young fellow out to impress the new girl in town.

As we watched the show Rodeo put on for his Princess, we laughed with surprise and joy. Where had this excited, suddenly *young* horse come from? Observing our boy, who'd been fading with loneliness and sorrow, become excited about a new companion blessed our day and brought gladness to our hearts.

While we thought we were rescuing our little Princess, she gave our Rodeo a new lease on life. His exuberance didn't last forever (because he was an old horse), but he had several more happy years with his new friend.

Sometimes a friend, companion, or a partner enters our life at just the right time to bring hope, joy, and second chances of love and life.

26

Even Cowgirls Grow Up

Dani Nichols

The first summer I worked as a wrangler, I came to the ranch with a big gelding I'd raised and broken myself. Hawkeye was beautiful, rippling with muscle with a coat, mane, and tail of glistening copper. He was tall and broad, built like a foundation quarter horse. Even an untrained eye could see how strong and fast he was, how in the right hands he would be the sort of horse who could climb mountains and chase cows without tiring, whose breadth and strength could be a real boon to any working ranch.

I was twenty years old, with more pride and hubris than sense, and I was surprised and dismayed when Jerry, my boss, told me to sell him. "He might kill ya," he said to me with concern in his eyes. "For certain, he'll get ya hurt."

Jerry, like most good dads, had very little grace for some lousy boyfriends of mine, and he told me to dump them on the spot. But he had almost infinite patience with horses, so his warning surprised me. I was desperate to prove myself as a real hand, so I wouldn't admit it, but Hawkeye scared me. He was "a lot of horse," as the cowboys say.

Hawkeye was breathtakingly handsome, and Jerry was right—dangerous. Nearly every day I felt him become a whirlwind of

141

horsehair and sinew erupting with cataclysmic force beneath me. Dust and gravel flew, and I heard the unsettled noises of the horses and riders around me. Every time, once we stopped, I'd learn that there'd been "a buck and a rear in there" and "you sat it fine"—the understated compliment of the day.

I was embarrassed, ashamed of my fear, how my heart pounded every time I swung my leg over him. I'd raised this colt from a foal and remembered him on lanky baby legs, running across the pasture in pure joy. I was fond of him and wanted to prove myself as a real horsewoman. But I didn't go against Jerry's advice. Reluctantly, I sold Hawkeye to a fearless young cowboy who promised to "ride the hide off him" and tried to forget my failure.

After all, I had enough to do without a big gelding to break in. I fixed fence and moved irrigation, worked cows and trained horses, offered trail rides to visitors, dug ditches, drove tractors. One day I led a trail ride up the mountain, and when we returned to the corral, the trail-riding vacationers waved their thanks and goodbyes and headed to the mess hall. Jerry was called away to some urgent matter on ranch property.

Shadows lengthened as eighteen horses stood patiently in their rigging—saddles, bridles, some with breast collars and second cinches. I gave a chagrined look around the corral and began untacking. Each horse got gentle pats and murmuring conversation as I moved through them, lifting heavy saddles and untying sweat-soaked cinches. They shook their manes in pleasure, nudged me gratefully with their noses, and gave deep, shuddering nickers as I passed by.

When Jerry came back, the tack was put away in the sheds and the horses were in the pasture, kicking up their heels and rolling in the lush grass, thrilled with their freedom. We often had companionable father-daughter talks by dusty twilight, resting tired arms on the fence rail and watching our beloved herd at leisure, long lines of irrigation water spraying life over the field and stars revealing themselves one by one.

But this night, there was no chatting about horse behavior or ranch-work problem-solving; rather Jerry gravely put his beefy hand on my thin, dusty forearm. "You know, Dani," he said, "it's amazing what you can do. Yer not very big, but you can do anythin' because of the power of yer mind."

I don't remember what I said in return. Knowing me, I probably laughed it off and pretended that his unwavering faith in me didn't shake me to my marrow. I tucked his words away in my heart and tried to believe that selling Hawkeye was not a sign of failure but of wisdom, that I'd get a second chance with a horse like him.

Sure enough, a couple of years ago I bought a muscled and skittish beautiful dun-colored quarter horse gelding. He was reminiscent of Hawkeye, my second chance at a horse I couldn't ride before but can now.

Of course, I called Jerry as soon as Buzz was in my pasture. "Guess what kinda horse I bought, and guess who he reminds me of," I cackled into the phone.

Jerry's chuckle was wheezier than it used to be, but he was as eager as ever to talk horses. "Lemme see," he said. "I betcha you got yourself another gelding?"

To my ecstatic "Bingo!" he replied with typical generosity, "Tell me all about it! By the way, I ever tell ya about the wild stud I had for a while, reminded me of that crazy horse o' yers . . . ?" And we're off, on another long and rollicking chat of horses and cows and wild rides, of missteps and mistakes and tall tales and derring-do. That's the beautiful thing about horses and the people who love them: they are changing and so are we. Every day is different, every ride is different, every relationship between horse and human is different. The stories are endless.

It's been twenty years since Jerry put his fatherly hand on my arm and told me I needed to sell my gelding for my own safety. He made the same gesture, so full of belief and kindness, when he told me I could do anything I put my mind to. I no longer see those two statements as contradictory but rather as complex and intricate. The reality is that good partnership is delicate. Strength is often best portrayed in gentleness; letting something go is frequently the way to persevere. Jerry taught me that horses can't be bullied but must submit of their own will, and scaring a horse or forcing it never leads to good outcomes for horse or rider. The wise horse person knows when to release control and when to offer compassionate leadership rather than mere dominance.

These days, I work as a horsemanship instructor, and I regularly find this dance of leadership and fear, wisdom and work ethic at play. "Breathe, relax your elbows, sit deep in your saddle," I tell nervous riders, a paradoxical piece of advice for those whose every instinct is telling them to hang on for dear life. Jerry's voice rings in my ears when self-doubt plagues me, when I have an unsatisfying ride or training session, when my horsemanship skills fail me, as they will from time to time. I've learned the hard way that both people and horses are complex and provocative, and sometimes the partnership between us isn't right. We humans, as the ones with checkbooks and choices, must have the maturity to admit it.

"You're better than you think you are," I tell my horsemanship students, because I know they need to hear it, just as I did. I know how to coach them through fear and insecurity, through failure and frustration, because I have felt those things too, because I also have longed for second chances with an animal I love.

I'm no longer an aggressive, secretly terrified cowgirl. I'm no longer a skinny desperate kid with longing in her eyes. I laugh and tell my horsemanship students that I don't bounce as well as I used to, but thank heaven, I no longer have to. Now I can ride most horses and train others to be better than they were.

I also see, as Jerry did, the necessary sale of a horse as an essential piece of animal husbandry, a way to steward opportunities for both horse and rider. I've coached more than one new horse owner to sell their animal and purchase one who might be a better fit for them. Rescue doesn't always come in a conquering hero or breaking the wild colt.

Sometimes rescue is the love of a wise father who helps you not break your neck. It's the advice that is laden with second chances and trying again, the reminder to our easily bruised hearts that life is long, and reconsideration is not failure.

I'm so glad my former selves come with me on every ride. The girl who took care of an entire trail string is there; the one who had a powerful mind hiding in her insecurity is also coming along; the one who loved horses enough to work twelve-hour days just to be with them joins us too. These cowgirls live within me and inform me. I ride my gelding with a wisdom borne from too many imprudent rides, rides Jerry gently and wisely taught me to work through or outsmart. The girls I have been come along as the mountains rise beneath our pounding hooves, and I'm grateful for second chances, for long twilights and hard work and the loving voice of a good father.

27

In the Depths of the Wash Racks

Nicole M. Miller

When I met him, he was the definition of tall, dark, and handsome. A long, black mane, dark muzzle, and sparkling red-bay coat of fur. His black tail dragged along the ground for at least a foot, and three of his pasterns were covered in short white socks. He had the pedigree and the regional halter championship to boot.

This was the purebred Arabian gelding who would take me to the next level in my horse showing career.

Before this horse, I'd endured the sour, cantankerous mare (who refused to load into a trailer) and the older, well-trained gray gelding (who had the habit of bucking randomly in the show ring). This horse, HMH Alegacy, or "Sigi" as he was called, was the next step.

There was just one catch.

Sigi was a bit . . . jumpy.

Well, jumpy might be understating it. He was downright scared of his own shadow.

I was sixteen years old—early in my horse career and so terribly naïve in all the ways of the world. Patience wasn't exactly one of the hallmarks of my personality. But Sigi was the horse my trainer felt would push me to the next step.

Oh, he pushed me all right.

From the very beginning, we butted heads, especially when he jumped at a blowing leaf onto my foot or panicked on the cross-ties. Instead of me better anticipating his reactions or working to build our trust as a team, I just got irrationally angry. I'd roll my eyes, scoff, and stomp around, which did little to ease his nervousness.

The unpredictability was irritating. One minute, we'd be doing great, and we'd sail through a class and win a ribbon. Another moment, he'd jump sideways and knock me over.

Sigi was the most expensive horse I'd purchased to date, and he was everything externally I'd wanted to enter the Arabian horse breeding shows. How could I possibly make this work? Months went by, and I really wasn't sure we'd reach an understanding. Had I made a terrible mistake?

But my trainer, who knew more about Sigi's background, reminded me to consider the full picture of this horse's life.

Sigi had been beaten as a young colt to look more "alert" and "wide-eyed" for the halter championships he'd been entered into. He was beaten with buckets while cross tied in the aisles, and he was even electrocuted in the wash racks. So his jumpiness wasn't some personality quirk. It was years of conditioning in the very worst way. My impatience, my anger, did nothing but continue this spiral for Sigi.

I had to rework my approach and better understand what this horse needed from me. And it was different than any other horse I'd worked with before. But if I did, perhaps we could really make strides.

Summer came around, and we boarded Sigi at my trainer's stables where I worked, so I could spend more time working with him during the height of show season. Cue the soundtrack to *Rocky*.

We went back to the basics—walking around and just getting to know each other. I found ways to adapt to his "crosstie phobia" that helped him feel safer in the aisles of the stables. I worked constantly with him to enter the wash rack, even if it was just for a little snack or treat.

By the end of the summer, we'd come a long way. We also hit up several local breed shows and had taken home as high as a third place ribbon. Considering I was "playing with the big boys" and not just competing against fellow 4-H'ers, I was mighty proud.

Something deep inside me changed as well. I was far more patient and a much better horsewoman by the end of that summer and in the years to come. Sigi taught me to read each situation with a different perspective and to appreciate how something that has been broken and shattered can be pieced back together with love and gold seams, like old Japanese pottery. Sigi became my greatest companion.

After high school, I dedicated years to finding him the next owner who would treasure him equally. He was a beautiful horse, and after placing a sale ad for him, I got many offers. But I evaluated each potential new home with a high standard. I knew Sigi needed someone with patience and a deep, deep understanding of his harrowed past. It was several years' journey to find him a safe and worthy home, but I wasn't going to let my partner and friend go into a situation I wasn't comfortable with, no matter the price tag.

Each horse leaves a unique hoofprint on your soul. But Sigi taught me more than any other horse I've owned. What's more, he truly overcame a lot of his fears and the edginess he'd had when I first bought him. By the end of my time with him, we were even successfully and without hesitation entering that dreaded wash rack and taking long, suds-filled showers.

With a little time, a little understanding, and a lot of patience, a life can be transformed. Mine. His. Those around us. I'm proud to have grown beyond who I was when I met Sigi, and I'm grateful for who he shaped me to be.

His registered name was HMH Alegacy, which has been burned into my mind. I don't recall the other registered names of my past horses quite in the same way. Because Sigi left a true legacy on me and my life. A legacy of deeper questioning, seeking. Of going beyond the surface reactions to consider the base fears and the scars unseen.

When I see a horse startle and jump, I give it a second look. When I feel people around me react in a surprising way, I wonder what in their past is driving their behavior. I thank Sigi for that.

He also left plenty of hoofprints on my toes—but who's counting?

28

When You Have a Dream

Jane Owen

My twelfth birthday wasn't what I expected. My dad gave me a present just from him. With a warm smile, he said, "This is something special I picked out for you."

I tore off the sparkling green paper and opened the box. Inside was a plastic horse, complete with a removable bridle and saddle. "Thanks, Dad," I mumbled.

He read my reaction. "I understand my gift seems juvenile." He paused. "This horse is meant to be a reminder for you."

He had my attention. I lifted the horse from the box and waited for his next words.

"I know you've wanted a real horse of your own." He glanced at my mom. "Your mother told me you prayed for one a couple of years ago."

I nodded.

Dad tapped the horse with his finger. His brown eyes met mine. "When you have a dream, don't let it go."

For a while after that day, the model horse stayed on my bedside table. Then teenage years flew by, followed by busy college days. After graduation, wedding plans consumed me. My childhood dream drifted away, along with Dad's encouraging words.

Fast forward to 1998—I pulled up to the barn where our youngest daughter stabled her horse and noticed an unfamiliar woman exiting the wide doorway. "Are you Jane?"

"Yes," I answered, getting out of my car.

She approached with a determined stride. "The stable owner said you might be interested in owning my Quarter-Morgan mare."

"Whoa! Terry told you that?"

"I'm Trish." She extended her hand. "Let me explain." With a fluttery smile, she continued. "I've had Lily two years—since she was ten. She's a lovely bay, very gentle and . . ."

"Then why are you selling her?"

"Well, that's just it. I'm not. Here's my dilemma. I've purchased a young Thoroughbred gelding. He's at another barn where I will continue his training." Her chin quivered. "Truthfully, I can't afford two horses. That's why I'm looking for someone who will take Lily and devote their time to her."

"Trish, I appreciate your situation, but . . ."

She stepped closer. "Will you at least meet Lily?" She looked away. "I haven't found anyone else . . ." The look on Trish's face defined *crestfallen*. "I don't mean to pressure you, Jane, but Terry urged me to talk to you."

"Okay. Just let me get a couple of apples from my car."

"Great!" I noticed Trish relax her shoulders.

As we entered the barn, she pointed to the right. "Lily's stall is over this way."

"My daughter Abbie's horse, Sara, is in the third stall straight ahead," I said. "I need to check on her first."

"I'd like to see Sara—if you don't mind. Terry told me how well you and Abbie care for her."

Trish stopped abruptly at Sara's stall. "Oh, she's an Arabian! Abbie must be a good rider."

"She is," I agreed, allowing Sara to nibble the apple from my palm. With a few juicy crunches, she finished her treat.

Though I resolved to politely refuse Trish's offer, I nevertheless said, "Now, let's see Lily."

151

My resolve vanished the instant Trish announced, "Here she is."

The memory of my childhood prayer flashed back: *Dear God, I want my own horse! It doesn't have to be beautiful—just mine. Please?* Now, my heart pounded as the passage of forty-four years brought me to this moment.

I rubbed Lily's nose, whispering, "Hello, girl." She nickered and lost me in her beautiful, soulful eyes. When she caught the scent of the apple in my pocket, the nuzzling began. With ease, she retrieved the Jonagold from the front pouch of my jacket.

Trish interrupted my thoughts. "Take your time with her. I'll be outside."

Lily nosed my jacket again. In a swirl of emotion, I wrapped my arms around her neck.

A few minutes later, I found Trish sitting on the weathered bench just outside the barn door. She scooted over as I sat down.

I stared out across the pasture, struggling to process the situation. Finally, I broke the silence. "When was Lily last vetted?"

"Two weeks ago. Here's the report."

I scanned the vet's paperwork. "This is certainly a favorable health assessment."

Trish's dark curls bobbed with each nod of her head. "I believe Lily will be perfect for you . . . if you decide to take her."

"I'll talk to my husband, Ron—and Terry too."

"Of course!"

"I'd also like Abbie to ride Lily."

She tilted her head toward me. "Don't you want to ride her too?"

"I do. But it's been forever since I've ridden a horse."

"Lily's a dream to ride. You won't have a problem with her."

A dream to ride. My dad's words welled up. *When you have a dream . . .*

I looked at my watch. "Oh, it's time to pick Abbie up from school."

Trish stood up. "Could we meet here on Saturday morning? About 10:00?"

"That sounds good. See you then."

When I picked thirteen-year-old Abbie up, she chattered about her school day. She tapped my arm. "Why are you so quiet?"

I smiled and made a U-turn, heading back to the barn. She grabbed the dash. "What's up, Mom? You act like you have a secret."

"I might," I answered, turning on the lane to the stable.

Through the barn doors, the scent of sweet hay greeted us. I took Abbie's hand. "Come this way."

When she saw Lily munching her alfalfa dinner, she said, "Ooooh. Who's this?" In record time, she heard my story. She scratched under Lily's chin. "What will Dad think of having two horses in the family?"

After dinner that evening, Abbie sat beside me on the couch, reading her dad's response as I unfolded the day's events. At the finish, Ron offered no immediate comment. Abbie looked at me and gave a slight shrug.

We both gave him a hug, though, when he said, "Let's all go Saturday." With the steady gaze of his blue eyes, he added, "But we won't make a rash decision."

Saturday morning arrived, and we found Trish had saddled Lily for us. She handed Abbie the reins. "Why don't you ride her first?"

"Sure!" Abbie beamed and led Lily to the pasture. Before mounting, she gently stroked Lily's forehead, talking softly to her. In the saddle, she urged Lily into a trot, then "kissed" her into a canter. I watched with delight to see our daughter and Lily moving together as one.

Abbie then leaned forward in the saddle and nudged Lily's sides, asking her to gallop. Lily didn't respond.

"Is something wrong, Trish?"

"Not at all. Lily just minds her own head."

"You mean she can be stubborn. Does she buck, kick, or bite?"

"Lily's never done any of that. She wouldn't gallop for me the first few times I rode her either. Once she adjusted to me, she was fine."

Abbie motioned for me to come into the pasture. "It's your turn, Mom. She's pretty responsive."

"But she didn't gallop for you."

"Lily needs some time to feel comfortable. That's all. I'll help you get on her."

The kid in me said, *Let me up in that saddle!* My adult side cautioned, *Are you sure you want to do this?* My kid-self won. Soon, the rocking chair motion of Lily's walk lulled me. When I asked her to trot, she didn't hesitate. I slowed her to a walk again and stopped her at the pasture gate. "Ron, Lily's ready for you!"

He shook his head, but Abbie took his arm, tugging him toward Lily. "Dad, get on and let her walk around the field." He consented, and we cheered as he made a couple of circuits.

As Ron dismounted, Terry arrived. "Trish," I said, "may Abbie continue riding while I talk to Terry?"

"Go ahead. I'll stay out here with her."

"Thanks," I said, motioning for Ron. "Terry," I called, "I want to talk to you!"

He flashed a big grin. "I see you've met Lily."

"Yes, but can you tell us anything we need to know about this arrangement?"

"You mean about Trish gifting Lily to you?"

"Exactly!"

He pulled at the brim of his cowboy hat. "Honestly, I was taken aback when Trish told me what she had in mind. I thought of you and Abbie right off though."

"Have you ridden her?"

"No, but I will if you want."

"How about now? I trust your experience and need your honest opinion."

I watched Terry ease Lily from the trot to the canter. "Ask her to gallop," I called. At first, Lily didn't take his request.

"Look, Mom!" Abbie climbed atop the fence. "Lily's galloping!"

Lily's graceful movement around the pasture and the cadence of her hooves made me tear up. When Terry reined her in and dismounted, he handed me the reins. "Jane, Lily is a seasoned mare you can trust."

I looked at Ron, who gave me a nod. I turned to Trish. "We'll be happy to take Lily."

Trish clasped her hands together. "I know you won't be disappointed."

Just a few weeks later, I decided on a solo afternoon ride. Sunshine and a tickling breeze enhanced our walk around the pasture trail. Lily cantered easily for me, encouraging my confidence. Then without warning, my fourteen-hands-high wonder broke into a full gallop. All I could do was hold on. I tried not to give way to panic, but going airborne struck me as a real possibility. Resisting the urge to jerk the reins back hard, I hollered, "Whoa, Lily! Slow up, girl!"

Chris, one of the barn hands, jogged up to the gate, calling, "Take her down easy, Jane. Hold her steady!"

Lily seamlessly reduced her speed and halted. I slid out of the saddle with great relief. Chris came to my side and took the reins. "Get back on Lily."

"I'm still shaking. Maybe another day."

Chris put the reins in my hands. "I've exercised Lily for Trish several times, and she's never galloped for me." She rested her hand on my shoulder. "This mare likes you and is beginning to trust you."

I took a deep breath. "You're right. Give me a leg up."

Chris walked beside us as we headed to a nearby round pen. "Now, relax, Jane. Trot Lily around a little. That way both of you can settle down. My advice? Keep riding. That will strengthen the bond between you and Lily."

A couple of months later, Lily and I joined three other riders on a riding trail. In the lead, an acquaintance rode a young Pinto named Jasper. The others followed along as Lily and I brought up the rear.

Suddenly, the trail turned to a steep incline. Jasper planted himself, refusing to climb. Clods of dirt tumbled down. That spooked the other two horses. The first tried to rear up, causing the one in front of Lily to draw back, threatening to bolt.

While those horses snorted, seeking escape, Lily stood her ground. I relaxed the reins, giving her permission to move out around the fray. Without hesitation, she took the lead and plodded up the rise. The timid steeds settled down and fell right in line behind Mama Lily.

One of the riders called, "Your mare is something! How did you train her to react like that?"

I ran my fingers through Lily's black mane. "I didn't. Her original owner told me she minds her own head. Today, I discovered what she meant."

After putting Lily in her stall that evening, I gave her an apple and let her find the carrot in my hip pocket. The closeness we shared flooded my heart.

One fall day, a riding friend invited Abbie and me to trailer our horses to an outdoor riding event for the local children's hospital. "They are sponsoring 'Happy Day' for kids and their parents," Diane explained. "The children will enjoy 'walking rides' around the venue."

Abbie and I nodded together. "We'd love to do this," I said.

Diane studied us both. "You know many of these children suffer severe illnesses. Their parents have signed waivers so their kids can participate, but . . . it could be a tough day for our hearts."

My heart couldn't resist. "Diane, a day of fun might make a great difference for these children."

How incredible that outing proved to be! For more than three hours, children of all ages took turns riding. Many parents walked alongside their children. One father remarked, "My boy hasn't smiled this much in a long while." Between rides, children pressed as close as possible to Lily. Their excitement shone in their eyes, and she added to their glee by nickering. I rejoiced that gentle Lily brought such joy to kids who also needed it.

Toward the end of the day, I noticed a little girl in leg braces. She stood with her mother, back from the other children.

I smiled. "Would you like to ride Lily?" She gave me a shy grin and looked up at her mother.

"Come meet my horse. You'll like her."

"Okay," she said, taking her mother's hand.

Her mom held her up to meet Lily face-to-face. "Tell Lily your name."

"Hi, Lily. I'm Coleen." She touched Lily's nose. "I'm eight."

I exchanged a smile with her mother. "Do you want to ride Lily now?"

"Yes," Coleen answered with a sweet voice.

My patient mare never flinched as Coleen's mom lifted her into the saddle. Cumbersome leg braces posed no problem for Lily.

On her third trip around, Coleen stretched herself forward on Lily's neck. "Hold on to her mane with both hands," I said, showing her how.

"Will that hurt Lily?"

I glanced across at Coleen's mother, whose eyes glistened. "No, Coleen. You won't hurt her at all."

"Lily, you're the nicest horsey!"

For two more poignant years, my incredible mare continued to prove she was the first and only horse I ever needed. I have an inkling my dad might say, "Your youthful dream faded away, but the Lord remembered and brought Lily to you right on time."

29

My Second Mariah

Catherine Ulrich Brakefield

My husband refused to take no for an answer. His strides ate up the dirt ahead of me. My emotions ricocheted around in my head, banging like a gong, and I dreaded what lay within the walls of that barn. Because I had seen it all before. Did I want to go through this again?

The barn door screeched open on rusty hinges, and I grabbed a shaky breath. The neighs of horses rippled through the centennial barn. What few windows the old barn had were covered with grit and spiderwebs. As my eyes adjusted from bright sunlight to the dismal dimness of the inner walls, horses of different sizes and colors stared at me. They were sheltered from the harsh elements of Michigan winters yet bound in their stalls with little care. Ears pricked forward; their large eyes watched me. Small stalls and smaller muddy paddocks packed with horses—that was the epitome of my worst nightmare, and a sight I had witnessed too often.

During the 1970s and '80s it seemed as if every horse owner with a mare was breeding her. Get-rich schemes of breeding grade mares with Arabian stallions had rippled through Michigan, and the phrase "backyard breeders" became a term every equine person heard repeatedly. There were more horses looking for homes than people wishing to burden themselves with the expense of owning a horse. My heart ached to take each one of these animals home with me. But that was a huge no from my husband.

Unbeknownst to me, Edward had already been to this farm once. Walking up and down the aisles, he was joined by the owner, who entered through a side door of the barn. Together they strolled the dirt aisleway, heads bent together.

Me, well, I spent my time petting each horse. I offered what I had, bits of carrots I grabbed for this excursion. As I walked down the aisle, I began counting. There had to be close to fifteen or twenty horses ranging in ages from mares to yearlings to weanlings. I hoped I had brought enough carrots for everyone. I might not be able to take every horse home, but at least I could offer them a treat, a friendly stroke, and a pat on the neck.

An old horseman's slogan I followed way back in my early teen years went something like this—if you get thrown off, climb right back on. It was a good motto. One I observed with all my mounts—as well as with life. Until now.

I had no slogan to lean upon when I lost my Mariah. I can't count the Western shows I watched when the cowboy had to shoot his loyal horse because it had broken its leg or had gotten shot. I totally empathized with the cowboy, or so I thought. Because when it comes to saying goodbye to your twenty-year-old buddy, reality hits you hard.

My horse's name came from the popular song "They Call the Wind Mariah." It was as if that song had been written for my horse, because oh, how she loved to run like the wind. She never appreciated the walking gait. She was always in a hurry to get where we were going.

Unfortunately, I was unaware that Mariah was hurting. She never refused me. She would still run after the other horses in the pasture. It took a bone shattering disease to make her quit, one that brought her up lame one summer day. I immediately phoned my veterinarian. He diagnosed it as laminitis.

That meant that Mariah had had an extreme fever in her foot that led to founder. My veterinarian mentioned it could have also been due to bad shoeing. All I learned about horses told me this never happened, so I asked for an X-ray. He took it and about five hours later I received a call. "She's got arthritis. Your mare's pastern coronary bone has completely disintegrated due to the disease."

The horse's pastern is that bone between the ankle (which is called the fetlock in a horse) and foot (called hoof in a horse). I was mortified—how had I not seen this coming?

"Cathy, over here."

I looked up. The owner and my husband found what they were looking for. I patted the last horse on her neck and walked forward to the owner of the barn. He was with a yearling.

"Meet Khalii Al Mariah," the owner said.

My heart skipped a beat. This farm was practically in our back-yard, and they had a horse named Mariah? A coincidence?

Some might have called Mariah a grade mare because she did not have papers. But she didn't need a pedigree. That upright tail, the eager eyes, and majestic neck told all who saw her she had either an Arabian mother or father.

As if the owner were reading my mind, he said, "And this little filly not only has papers but a pedigree a mile long. She's the grand-daughter of a syndicated Egyptian stud named Shaikh Al Badi."

I stepped forward. She was tall for a yearling. Her thick black mane and tail complemented her blood-red coat, and she was long-legged but not gangly. Her conformation was superb. Her big coal-colored eyes looked at me. She hesitated to walk forward as if half-afraid of striking up a relationship only to be disappointed.

I could see her stall hadn't seen a pitchfork in months. I coaxed her by holding out a carrot. She came hesitantly. That's when I noticed her hooves badly needed trimming. One hoof had curled upward, in a sort of elfin look. Her fetlocks were angled, lower to the ground than they should be, which showed weak pasterns, probably due to the inch or more shavings mixed with manure on the floor of her stall and the lack of exercise. She could possibly have thrush too. She would require corrective trimming so her foot would not grow abnormally and then corrective shoeing. Plus she needed a stall with a clay floor. We had just the one for her. I hoped it wasn't too late for her to gain strength in those pasterns. I needed to help this yearling *now*. Waiting could be catastrophic for her. Was this a chance to redeem myself for having missed Mariah's illness? To help this horse that possibly would not have a chance otherwise?

"Yeah, I noticed that too." Edward bent close. "You think we can fix her up?"

I didn't know. But if I said so, my husband would not chance the money to buy her. I nodded.

"Okay if we bring her out of the stall?"

"Sure, but my daughter actually owns these horses. I've informed her she has to either sell them or find a place for them before she gets married." The man shook his head. "I don't need more work. The guy we hired to do the stalls always has an excuse not to show."

I felt Mariah's excitement leaving her dark stall for a look-see outside. She pranced around in a high-stepping trot with her little yearling wisp of a tail flipping over her rump. I could tell she would be like my previous horse, always eager to get where we were going. Edward could tell it was love at first sight. But I remained hesitant. I could only imagine what the price tag for this filly was.

You need to know a little bit about my husband. He has deep Southern roots and is a negotiator at heart. Some men love to whittle pretty things out of wood. My husband loves to whittle down prices.

The back door of the farmhouse banged open and shut, and the daughter walked over, holding in her hands a price sheet. "That's the horse you're interested in?"

"Yes, ma'am," my husband said.

She consulted her paper and said, "I already have a buyer for her. He's going to try and get the money up for her in a couple of months."

That didn't impress her dad. He boomed out in his impressively bold voice, "Remember what I say, money talks—show me the green, or you can walk!"

"Dad. You know I don't like that saying," the daughter said.

"Did he give you any cash down?" her dad asked.

"No, but—"

"Then this here little filly is still for sale." Her father considered the subject closed. He turned toward my husband and said, "So what's your final offer?"

"Let's walk." My husband and the owner strolled off. They bickered and laughed and bickered again, and soon I had myself a new horse.

Only that wasn't the end of it. When my father learned the owner also had the daughter of Shaikh Al Badi, my father had to have her. The mare's name was Kashana, and she was in foal. So we left the owner's barn with not one but two and a half horses that day, and I reveled in the knowledge that we had saved three horses. I knew the newborn foal would also need special attention to its pasterns and hooves.

The next day, after her first trimming, we walked Khalii Al Mariah around the pasture, then let her go on her own. She took off at a run and hit a guidewire to a telephone pole and did a flip! You'd think she would've learned her lesson and would lie there so we could come help her. But she jumped up and started running again and hit the metal fence. What was wrong, was she blind? Then I noticed she didn't hit the wooden fencing.

Then it dawned on me. Her knowledge of fencing apparatus was equivalent to a newborn foal. I could have kicked myself. Of course. She'd never been in an area with metal fencing before. Because the wire is thin, and sunlight penetrates around it, newborn foals don't consider it inhibiting—until they collide with the thin metal. Why, just by looking at her hooves, I should have realized the truth.

"By the looks of it, she's never been in a ten-acre pasture before in her life," Edward said.

I nodded in agreement. "All she knew were small wooden paddocks. But just look at her perseverance. Instead of staying down, she jumped right back up and tried again. Falling the second time didn't faze her—she kept on. She's determined to see how fast those long legs of hers can go."

"Well, she's found their use and is making up for lost time," Edward said with a chuckle.

The next day went better, and she adapted to our herd. Having her mother there helped.

"She loves it here." I leaned over and rested my arms on the wooden fence, watching her run, that little tail, like an exultant flag, flowing in the breeze of her galloping hooves. The other horses would take off after her, joining her in her victory gallop.

Every morning when we put our horses out, Mariah would start off at a dead run. Those long legs of hers outran them all. She'd finish off with a high-stepping trot. Tail up and neck arched, she was poetry in action. I felt both awed and amazed. She was so happy to be out of that dark stall and in a pasture where she could run to her heart's content.

After losing my first Mariah, I was planning to stay down. To quit. But like this new Mariah, I wouldn't be happy living a sheltered life without sunlight or space to stretch my legs—or never being on the back of one of these majestic animals again.

The months sped by, and before we knew it, it was time to train Mariah. She proved to be athletically adaptable for any show class we cared to enter her in. The first show was with her mother when Mariah was two years old. We entered her in a fitting and showing class at the State Fair Grounds in Michigan. I rode her mother in a saddle seat class. Both horses did very well.

Mariah was full of surprises. I learned that the most stunning attribute of the Arabian breed is you never break an Arabian. You become friends first, and then you train them and hope they pick you as their rider. If you want to get their top performance, heed their preference and watch the fascinating change to their temperament.

When training Mariah for cross-country riding, I decided to ride our quarter horse named Candy, thinking she'd be the best pick as a mentor for the young and inexperienced three-year-old Mariah. After all, the quarter horse breed was more cold-blooded and dependable, not like the hot-blooded Thoroughbred and Arabian breeds. I needed to start Mariah off slowly, without anything getting her nervous or uptight riding cross country.

All went well until I trotted around a corner, and a flock of pheasants flapping their wings loudly chose to soar above my head. Candy reared straight up, pawing the air. Mariah stood still, looking at the disturbance, then at Candy. This calmness was just a sample of Mariah's capabilities when she was trail-riding.

Then our new horseback riding venue became foxhunting. Mariah outgalloped everyone and became our fearless leader that led us into thickets and swamp water without a pause. Her hooves tapped to their own music. She never shied at anything, and she loved seeing the world unobstructed by the rump of another horse. Mariah could clear a three-foot coop with no problem and cover the endless miles of countryside with ease. Our other Arabians would follow their bold leader through anything.

The years marched forward. My children are now grown, with children of their own. They, too, grew up to be equine riders. I often visualize Khalii Al Mariah on that first day we watched her run to her heart's content. Her legs barely touching the ground, she seemed to fly across those hills. Oh, how she loved to run! We were there to help her in her journey with blacksmiths and veterinarians so she could enjoy what she loved most—galloping like the wind.

I gave Mariah a chance to run. And she gave me another chance to love.

30

From Cows to Kids

Carmen Peone

After a hard career of chasing cows on the Colville Indian Reservation in Eastern Washington, Mocco came home. Not to my home at first, but to one of my grandsons—a grandson who, unlike his mom and dad, just wasn't into horses.

And I had a need. A very special need. You see, my other grandkids wanted a chance to ride, and neither of my horses was kid friendly.

Our child-caring mare had passed away a few years earlier, and the pony I'd bought was too much for my little cowpokes to handle. After selling the pony, I prayed for direction. Get another horse or not? Does someone have one we can borrow?

Then it dawned on me that our ranching son had horses standing around in the pasture. Eating. Sleeping. Doing . . . well, not much of anything except keeping the cows company.

I loved earthy-scented horses, and I wanted to pass on my adoration to my grandkids. To share the human-horse bond with the next generation—a legacy of sorts. Surely, one of our son's horses held the answer to my prayers. Right?

The next spring, I figured the time was ripe. Said grandson now preferred to ride in the side-by-side with Grandpa, which made

165

a pretty strong case for his horse, Mocco, to come to my little ranch for a summer.

Feeling giddy, I swooped in and made my case. "I'll provide feed and shoeing and pay any vet bills that might occur while Mocco stays at my place."

When my son pinned a "you're outta your mind" look at me, my heart dipped. Then it climbed back into my chest and purred when my grandson piped up, a wide grin on his face, "Grandma, you can borrow Mocco anytime."

Yeehaw! I had the boy on my side. All I needed was for his dad to agree. So I pressed on until he reluctantly agreed to let the aged horse come to my place for a spell after I assured him that I only wanted to *borrow* the horse, not keep him.

Once he moved onto our 140-acre horse ranch, the leggy bay began to settle in next to my two geldings. The next day, I tried to catch him. Then tried again. And again. I knew Mocco had been a loner in his previous herd (yes, you read that correctly) and hated to be caught. Probably hated the grueling hours and rugged terrain he used to have to cover while on a working cow ranch in Eastern Washington and Canada with his previous owner. Though he'd been retired for a few years, he still ran when he caught sight of a halter.

So I put him in my small arena and went to work. Forty-five minutes later, I caught him. Thanks to a technique I'd learned from renowned horse trainer Julie Goodnight, the cat-and-mouse chase ended. Mocco, the tall bay quarter horse, could now be caught. Whew.

Eventually, I grew a deep bond with him through feeding, grooming, and loving on him. Some days I'd simply wrap my arms around his soft neck and inhale. If only I could bottle that scent. It didn't take long for what the two of us shared to transfer to four of my younger grandkids as they, too, fed, groomed, and loved on old Mocco.

And when it became time to ride, Mocco walked around the arena, maneuvering around and over obstacles, taking extreme care with the little ones. He taught my young grandkids how to ride. Taught them about teamwork and horsemanship as we worked with poles, cones, barrels, and horse-sized teeter-totters and bridges.

More than once, tears of joy leaked from this granny's eyes as I witnessed low self-esteem bloom into confidence from riding. Nervous eyes turned bright, and chins raised up. And big smiles made the extra time and effort in my already busy schedule worth it. Well worth it.

When each of those four children proved they could control and stop old Mocco, we hit the trail. Again, hot and happy tears slid from my eyes a time or two because one of my dreams had come true—trail-riding with my grands.

My heart swelled as one of my granddaughters trotted him around pine and fir trees, talking the entire time because she, too, was in heaven. When my eight-year-old grandson proved he could handle Mocco, we rode around our property. The smile on his face thrummed my heartstrings. As did his professing, "I did it, Nahnah!" (short for Kocknah, a Salish word for paternal grandmother).

Yes, he did. And this grandson is now encouraging his cousin to ride by herself so she too can hit the trail along with the rest of us.

Who would have thought one old horse would take care of so many kids? He now lets them catch and groom him. The girls love playing with his coarse mane and tail. I still have to put the saddle on his back, but they do the rest.

At twenty-seven, Mocco lives here and will remain here until he passes on. He has the run of the ranch. Old and thin, he gets as much hay as he wants with Haystack added to his grain twice a day and a warm blanket during the icy winter months. He's not much of a loner anymore either as he and my old paint gelding have formed a bond.

I'm not sure Mocco realizes how much he's done for my family. Or perhaps he does. Either way, this year, it's my granddaughters' summer to shine. Thanks to the old bay's caretaking, they have gained enough confidence to move on to my tall half quarter horse, half Morgan gelding. At ten, he's faster and harder to handle than

Mocco. But they've proved they can take the reins and lead with assurance.

I don't know how much more time we'll have with Mocco. But while he's here and able, we'll continue to make lasting memories. I'm thankful for the time we've had with him and have to agree with Winston Churchill: "There is something about the outside of a horse that is good for the inside of a man."

Or in this case, a woman and her grandchildren.

31

Apache's Conversion

Capi Cloud Cohen

"When you get home, tell your mom to come to the corral," Mrs. Pollard said after I had hung up my saddle and bridle following our afternoon ride. I was headed for my motorbike and the dirt road that doubled as a racetrack, the first leg of my journey toward home. I looked at her with a puzzled expression. It was time for dinner, homework, baths, and bed. No one ever went to the corral in the evening.

"Something is wrong with Apache. He hasn't eaten his food."

Apache was Mom's horse. He was what my dad called "a mean ol' cuss," and Mom was the only one with the nerve to ride him.

Apache's nasty personality was legendary in our local riding group, a bunch of elementary school students and the moms who kept us in line. Three afternoons a week and Saturdays were riding days. The horses grazed in the Venezuelan grasslands overnight and while we attended school. They were rounded up and brought to the corral by a weathered, bow-legged cowboy named Don Venado every afternoon. The horses knew where each belonged, and they habitually headed into their assigned slots, ready for their daily meal under the corrugated tin roof that covered the stalls.

Apache's stall was the first on the left. The one next to him stayed vacant, for good reason.

As we trickled into the corral after school and early on Saturdays, stopping to collect brushes, combs, saddles, and bridles from the tack room, we hugged the right side of the aisle separating the two rows of stalls that faced each other. Apache made a habit of lunging, teeth bared, at anyone who might get too close to him on their way to their own horse. We learned the hard way to give him a wide berth, whether in the stalls or on the trails. His kicks were as accurate and as nasty as his bites.

Apache was the fourth descendant of Spanish horses to join our family. When we moved from Utah to this small Venezuelan mining town south of the Orinoco River and showed interest in learning to ride, Mom and Dad began looking for horses for my brothers and me. One by one, Indio, Tonka, and Apollo came to us. Then Mom decided that she wanted to resurrect her childhood riding skills and join us on the Saturday rides through the countryside. Mostly I think she felt sorry for Mrs. Burdan and Mrs. Pollard, herding so many kids and horses every week.

When Apache arrived on the scene, there were no external indications that he had been treated badly. But his hateful belligerence made us suspect that he hadn't come from a happy home. Mom was determined to win him over with kindness, and eventually they came to an uneasy truce. She never walked behind him when brushing his hindquarters or tail, and she always watched the whereabouts of his feet, lest he try to stomp on hers. She had someone hold his halter rope when she cleaned his hooves, fearing he would use the opportunity to take a chunk from her back or shoulder.

Saddling him was a tug-of-war. He filled his lungs with air and held his breath, making it impossible to tighten his cinch. Mom would pull and strain, holding onto the end of the strap, waiting until he had to exhale so she could quickly tug the cinch again. At the end of the battle, Mom climbed into the saddle. To his credit, he never did try to throw her. And he always ate his food.

That night, after I delivered my message, Mom wolfed down her dinner, pulled on her jeans and boots, and headed to the corral, leaving Dad to deal with the evening routine alone. Mrs. Pollard was walking Apache in circles around the riding ring.

"Anne," she said, "I'm pretty sure he has colic. His stomach is hard and hot. He hasn't eaten. The only thing we can do is keep him on his feet and hope his guts will start things moving in the right direction." She handed Mom the rope and final instructions before heading home to feed her own family. "I'll be back in a little while, and we'll give him an enema if nothing has changed. Just keep him on his feet. Keep him walking."

Mom and Mrs. Pollard spent the entire night with Apache. There was no veterinarian within hundreds of miles, so they were on their own, doing the few things they knew to do. They walked him for hours, they gave him an enema that did nothing to help, they struggled to keep him on his feet, and they prayed desperate prayers. Eventually he refused to walk any farther and he lay down, eyes glazed in pain. His bloated belly hurt when they touched it. He moaned when he moved. They struggled uselessly to get him on his feet again.

As dawn approached and Apache showed no signs of improvement, Mrs. Pollard said, "I'm so sorry, Anne. We need to let him go. I'll go home to get my gun. We really have no other choice."

"I know," Mom replied, brokenhearted that her "mean ol' cuss" of a horse wasn't going to survive this bout of colic.

While Mrs. Pollard was gone, Mom stroked his sleek brown neck and poured her heart out to Apache, telling him that she was sorry that they hadn't been able to help him, that she was sorry to lose him, despite his cantankerous personality. And she begged him to get up.

Somehow something miraculous happened in those quiet early morning moments. Apache lifted his head for the first time in hours. He looked at Mom and he tried to stand. When Mrs. Pollard returned, he was still trying to get up. The three of them, Mom, Mrs. Pollard, and Apache, worked together to get him on his feet. Two sleep-deprived moms and a weak, exhausted horse walked slowly, hopefully, in circles in the riding ring again. Gradually, as they plodded, Apache's body set itself to rights.

In the days that followed this long, awful night, we noticed a change in Apache's personality. His near-death experience had seemingly purged him of his nastiness. Maybe he knew that he had almost come to the end of his days, and this was his chance at redemption. So, he thanked the women who spent that night trying to save his life by never kicking or biting anyone again. He was, indeed, a new horse.

32

Never Too Late

Barbara Ellin Fox

"He got raked down the back legs in the race today. And he's lame. Been that way a while." The middle-aged man with a protruding stomach and a rumpled tan shirt off-loaded a bright chestnut horse from the trailer. He handed me the horse's lead rope and a file folder, slammed the trailer gate shut, then scurried into his truck and left.

The horse stood rock still on the dirt drive facing my Kansas barn. Sweaty tension wafted off his body like heat from asphalt on a hot summer day. I'd never seen him before, and he didn't know me from any other groom or handler he'd had on the racetrack. Wary eyes gazed at his surroundings as he took in a new barn, an unfamiliar group of horses, and another stop on his life trip from trainer to trainer, track to track, race to race.

I glanced at my watch. Two hours until lunch. That left the afternoon to settle this animal before the after-school riding students arrived. They would instantly adopt this new end-of-the-line racehorse into our family at Golden Meadows Equestrian Center. Watching me rehab a horse increased their horsemanship education. And even the smallest pony rider dreamed of one day riding a Thoroughbred.

My assistant took the lead while I looked through the file folder. Familiar Jockey Club registration papers with the name Colonel Tuleg caught my eye. I flipped the sheet and counted nine past owners who'd given up on the horse during the last six years. I shuffled through health papers, then pulled out the record from today's race. They'd entered him as Colonel Two-legs, an obvious testament to his lameness. My stomach churned. Yet they'd still given him drugs and forced him to run. Tremors moving along his jugular groove, his increased pulse, and his clammy coat showed they hadn't yet worn off.

I set the folder aside and began an examination of the horse, speaking to him in soothing tones. His short tail didn't reach his hocks, and deep red scrapes covered the insides of his back legs. Racehorses measure how close they are to the horse in front of them by the length of the opponent's tail. Today's challenger misjudged, and his hooves raked the skin from this horse's legs. It's a wonder Colonel stayed on all four feet to the finish line. I continued my examination and bent down to wrap a hand around his left front fetlock. A puff of wind ruffled my hair as his hind foot flew over my head. I'd found his pain point.

Once he'd rested and the drugs worked out of his system, Colonel became a cooperative horse. He never threatened to hurt me again. We doctored a fractured sesamoid bone in his front leg, and then he spent lots of time turned out to pasture while the leg healed.

A colt bred for racing goes into training at a year and a half old when horses of other breeds are hanging out in pastures playing with their buddies. Carrying a rider, learning how to bolt out of starting gates, and running as fast as he can around the track becomes a racehorse's life. He doesn't enjoy the pasture on his days off. He trains, races, and stays in a stall. Giving the OTTB (off-track Thoroughbred) access to pasture, horsey friends, and grass a little at a time is restorative. Watching them learn to be a horse is both heartwarming and interesting.

Colonel's personality blossomed as his pasture time increased, and he experimented with things he might have done as a colt. We learned not to leave a lead rope on the pasture fence or Colonel would swipe it. He'd grasp the rope in his teeth, then flip his nose up and down, twirling his toy like a cowboy's lasso, often while rearing on his hind legs. Then he'd let the rope go mid-spin, watch it fly into the field, and race after the projectile the way a dog plays fetch. To keep track of equipment, we gave him his own ropes to play with. If he found the hose unhooked from the spigot, he'd twirl huge loops. Not as easy to toss as a lead rope. When the loops fell over his head and neck, he'd give a goofy look as if to say, "Well, that didn't work."

As a safety measure, I kept a halter and rope for each horse hanging on their stall near the opening for feed so that if we had an emergency, we wouldn't waste precious time searching. Misplaced equipment frustrated me to blue blazes, so when Colonel's halter and rope disappeared, I accused the kids who frequented the barn of using things and not putting them back. I hung a new halter on Colonel's stall, and it disappeared. This happened multiple times.

Masses of cobwebs in barn rafters are a fire hazard, and although we put the dirty job off, we cobwebbed twice a year. Imagine my surprise when I entered Colonel's stall with my broom, looked at the ceiling to assess the work, and spied four halters with lead ropes dangling from the crossbeams. Colonel had enjoyed his twirling game inside, and I owed a couple of kids an apology.

Out of twenty thousand Thoroughbred foals born each year, two-thirds of them will start in a race by the time they are five years old, with a third racing as two-year-olds. If a horse wins, his value skyrockets in the eyes of the trainer and owner. The bright stars might be lucky and retire to the breeding shed. Most Thoroughbreds end up like Colonel, who started out winning, then wore down, went lame, and competed in cheaper races against slower horses. He moved from fancy big East Coast racetracks to smaller Midwest dirt tracks until there were no more places for him.

Sometimes a trainer or owner goes broke. I've been to racetracks where horses are left behind in stalls with their registration papers tacked to the front. Whoever pays the horse's bill to get him off the racetrack can have him. Fifteen thousand end-of-the-line Thoroughbreds go to slaughter each year. The lucky ones get a chance at a second career. Bert, another OTTB, came to us after many homes and multiple second chances at new careers. When his West Coast racing career ended, they trained him as a jumper. After a few years on the California show circuit, a bad jumping accident injured Bert, and he lost his nerve. Next, he learned dressage. After Bert reached an advanced level as a dressage horse, his owner gave up riding and donated him to a private school in the Southwest. He'd become a tax write-off.

We needed a tall horse for my daughter to take to summer camp. My friend, who administrated at the school, offered Bert as a loaner horse. She said, "He's not pretty, and he isn't happy in the herd at school. I don't know if you can get him to jump, but he's tall."

Although thin from competing with other horses for food, and nervous from moving, the snow-white, seventeen-hand horse defined Thoroughbred. Smooth muscle and long legs gave elegance to his big strides and springy trot. He hated jumping, and his lack of flexibility proved that much time had passed since he'd practiced dressage. His stoic personality told me stress had driven him into a mental shell. Old horsemen say if you want to see the soul of a horse, look into his eyes. Bert's were hives of worry. He internalized the same way some people do.

When camp ended, I had to choose between taking Bert home or sending him back to the school. We had nine horses at our house, and I couldn't justify taking another, so I gritted my teeth and told my friend to load him into her trailer. She said, "We don't have a student for him this year. That means the horse administrator will send him to the dealer."

An older horse going to a dealer was synonymous with a trip to a slaughterhouse. The thought of any horse having such a horrid end gutted me. But Bert? I cried, and my husband loaded him into our trailer. We took him home.

Bert had a hard time adjusting to his new life. He worried about who would handle him next or where he might go. He reminded me of shelter dogs we'd had. Sometimes they took months to settle in and trust they were home.

Owners had entered Bert in races from the age of two years old, then competed him in jumping and dressage. Horse shows made Bert shake with anxiety, so we didn't ask him to compete. Plus, he'd developed ulcers, which caused him to colic multiple times. The big white horse had paid an enormous price to do the bidding of people over the years.

Bert became my horse. I spent hours grooming him, and when we rode together, I let him relax. As he gained back his confidence and became limber, he showed me his advanced dressage movements, and we even jumped small obstacles. I loved watching Bert gallop around our field or stop and rear colt-like to play with the other horses. He felt secure and lived out his old age as a normal horse.

The same way these horses had a second chance to enjoy their best life, so can people. My heart ached when the time came to leave my life's work and retire from training horses and teaching riders. There is still so much to do, so many horses needing a future. My world has always been about the horses, and each one I've known has contributed to the person I am today. They have been my passion since childhood and my career for more than half a century.

Now their lessons and memories have opened the door for my second career as an author. Instead of influencing one student or one horse at a time, I can reach a hundred thousand people with the message about horses and their value. My second career has given me a new way of relating to people. Through stories, these amazing animals can help others find their happily ever after.

I never dreamed a second chance could be better than the first. But it is.

FULFILL YOUR HORSE DREAM!

Are you a horse lover who longs for an opportunity? Maybe you rode as a child, then had to live life as an adult and always wished to get back to horses. Or perhaps you've always loved horses and could never enjoy them in person. Don't give up. There is time to fulfill your dream. If you are ten years old, twenty, or sixty-five, you can still enjoy horses. There are many avenues for horse lovers of all ages and experience. Offer to help with chores or grooming at a rescue. Donate to a shelter. Learn to be a side-walker at a therapeutic riding program.

If you love the idea of adoption and don't have a place for a horse, consider sponsoring one through a rescue. Perhaps you have a place to keep a horse and are more interested in relationship building than riding. Then adopt an unrideable horse.

If you are a beginner horse person, find an instructor in your area who can teach you the basics of handling and riding. When you feel confident with a lesson horse, you'll be more prepared to take on a horse of your own. (A tip: Because of their size and exuberance, an OTTB—off-track Thoroughbred—may not be the best choice for a first-time horse owner.)

Maybe you'll do a partial lease on a school horse. Or perhaps you'll buy or adopt with a friend. Often a riding program will have a group of ladies who hang out, talk horses, and enjoy each other's company.

Remember that horse rescues have all types and levels of horses who need caring, forever homes.

—Barbara Ellin Fox

33

Matched Pairs

Lonnie Hull DuPont

When I was a teenager, I worked summer jobs—babysitting, house-cleaning, clerking at a small grocery store. One summer, I picked and planted strawberries for a farmer. This was hot and boring work, to be sure. Picking the berries was tolerable (and popping a fresh one in the mouth was bliss). But planting them was the kind of repetitive task I found myself doing in my sleep all night long.

I cannot recall what contraption we sat on to do this, but another teenager and I were pulled around the fields, row after row, and we'd pinch plants into an archaic mechanical wheel that dug the plants into the ground. Around and around. So slow. So hot. And the farmer himself was a bit of a taskmaster.

The cool thing for me was that we were not pulled by a tractor but rather by a matched pair of workhorses. This farm was the only one I knew that still used these large and strong draft horses in the fields. I didn't know what kind they were, but they were dark and mythically huge. They wore blinders, and they whisked their long tails to swat at bugs. Although I mostly only saw the south side of those beasts, so to speak, they were wonderfully alive. No diesel smells as they plodded along. The farmer spoke very little to them, but they knew what was required, responding occasionally with a snort.

I grew up around horses. We had one or a few at any given time, and neighbors also had them, but I never had experience with draft horses until the strawberry fields. The farmer's team made such an impression on me that for years I paid an entrance fee to the county fair simply to see the Percheron horses. I have always gathered calm and happiness around animals, and at the county fair, I would spend hours in the barns, simply watching those mighty Percherons. I found them regal and beautiful and so soothing to be around.

Although I lived in my mother's house in the country, I spent most weekends at my father's house in the city. Across the street lived five delightful cousins. The oldest and only boy was nicknamed Hoddy. He was very sweet to me, his little cousin who was many years younger.

I remember when I was about four and he seventeen, I sat on a tricycle, watching him paint a garage. He asked me if I understood why we were cousins.

I said I did.

He said, "So how is it that we're cousins?"

I said, "Your daddy and my daddy are brothers."

He thought I was brilliant for knowing that. He showed me off to his buddies: "Tell them why we're cousins."

"Your daddy and my daddy are brothers."

Hoddy beamed. "Isn't she smart?"

Of course, I always liked him. But in a divorced family, we didn't see each other much after I grew up and no longer spent visitation weekends with Dad. Then Dad moved out of town, so I only saw my cousins at weddings and funerals. Except for a couple of reunions, it has been that way ever since.

So last year I was especially saddened to learn that my big-brotherly cousin was ill with cancer, and not long after diagnosis, he died. The funeral was about a hundred country miles away from where I live, and I made plans to attend by myself. At the time, I was undergoing physical therapy for a very painful back issue. It was the kind of thing where for the entire summer, I could only sit in one specific chair at home, and I avoided leaving the house. I was nervous about sitting somewhere with this ailing back. But I didn't want to miss paying my respects and seeing my cousins, so I cancelled a physical therapy appointment to attend the funeral.

With my heated car seat on my back, I drove alone through some glorious summer farms. The town itself was small, and the church was a handsome stone building, the service packed with people. Hoddy had been much loved.

Since I'd not seen him very often in my adult years, I didn't know everything about him. One thing I learned in the obituary was that my city cousin had become a horse man. The name of his horse (and his dogs) made the obituary, where I also learned that he participated in his county's mounted posse, riding in local events and parades. His love of horses seemingly had become a substantial part of his life. This was news to me.

I arrived at the church, found a pew in back, and waited for the service to begin. My back started hurting right away with an occasional spasm. I stood in the back, then sat back down. I found a pillow. I stood back up. Sat back down. Walked in the back of the crowded church for a while. It soon became clear that this was not going to work, and the day was just beginning. I couldn't afford to have spasms kick in this far from home. Reluctantly, I left the funeral and headed to my car—and my heated seat.

I felt sad as I drove out of the lovely little town and away from my cousins I so seldom saw. There was no highway between Hoddy's town and mine, only two-lane country roads. As I headed south toward home, the sun was midway down the bluest western sky. Everything I passed was green and lush and verdant. It was the kind of summer light when all that green seemed almost gold.

I continued thinking about Hoddy. I wished life had allowed us all to stay closer. I considered pulling over to check in with my feelings and to offer a prayer to honor my cousin.

Then I saw movement in the field on my right. Way at the back of the field, I could see a team of horses plowing, headed my way, moving in a small cloud of dust. They were steered by an Amish man walking behind them, holding long leathers. I had passed this farm on the way up and noticed it because it stretched from the road on to the west like an ocean.

I pulled over to the side of the road next to the fence and watched as the team made its way straight toward me. I was stunned by the magnificence of an animated, matched pair of draft horses. And they were palominos, my favorite look in a horse—golden body, blondish-white mane and tail. Their pacing was rhythmic, deliberate, efficient as they plowed together in a straight line toward me. Even though they were draft horses hard at work, they almost seemed to be prancing. Their long wheat-colored manes and tails blew in the breeze. They tossed their huge heads as they came closer.

I stayed in my car, turned off the engine, and opened the windows, mesmerized by the horses' size and beauty. They eventually came right to the fence and paused. The Amish farmer, who looked tiny next to them, steered them into a broad right-hand turn, kind of like a semitruck might make in traffic. Now I could see the curved sides of their shimmering cinnamon bodies pass by the fence. We were only a few yards away from each other. They turned again and headed back across the field, away from me. The farmer acknowledged me with a nod and continued with his work.

This all took some time. I found myself in a calm state—even my back pain subsided for a bit. I felt that this unexpected moment with the matched pair of palominos was a gift. It softened my sadness, and it helped me honor my cousin. Hoddy and I both loved animals. I'd always taken solace in them, and I suspect he did too. Now for a moment, a gorgeous team of horses in a June breeze bridged a gap of sorts and took away some of the sting of not being with family. Instead, I was with creation. I was grateful. It was as perfect as it could be.

I watched those long blond tails swish back and forth as the team moved away from me across the field. I waited as the horses became smaller and smaller until I could no longer see them. Then I stayed quiet for a time before I started the car back up and drove home.

Hoddy had always made his kid cousin feel special.

For a while, I felt that way again.

About the Contributors

DeVonna R. Allison is a renaissance woman who has held many professions, from stay-at-home mom, librarian's assistant, church secretary, and United States Marine. She is a writer and a woman of faith who makes her home in Central Florida with her husband/life partner, Earl.

Catherine Ulrich Brakefield is the author of *Wilted Dandelions*, *Swept into Destiny*, *Destiny's Whirlwind*, *Destiny of Heart*, *Waltz with Destiny*, and *Love's Final Sunrise*. She has been published by Guideposts Books, CrossRiver Media, Revell, and Bethany House. Catherine and her husband of fifty years have two adult children, four grandchildren, four Arabian horses, two dogs, five cats, and seven chickens. See www.CatherineUlrichBrakefield.com for more information about her.

Deborah Camp is an award-winning writer of cat-themed stories, and she has authored hundreds of nonfiction articles on topics including entrepreneurship, humor, pets, and travel. Her stories have been published in *Second-Chance Cats* and *The Cat in the Christmas Tree*. She is a retired professor of graduate business studies who currently works as a freelance writer and editor. She lives in Memphis, Tennessee, with her husband and three cats.

Capi Cloud Cohen is a blessed daughter, wife, mom, and grand-mother who writes stories, bakes cookies, and sews quilts and clothes in Tennessee. She is so thankful her parents were adventurous, as her experience of growing up in Venezuela shaped her life. Her children and six of her nine grandchildren speak Spanish with her and with each other. Capi's stories also appear in Chicken Soup for the Soul books.

Lonnie Hull DuPont is an award-winning poet, editor, and author of several nonfiction books. Her poetry can be read in dozens of literary journals, and her work has been nominated for a Pushcart Prize. She is a member of Cat Writers' Association and Dog Writers Association of America, and her nonfiction is frequently about animals, including her memoir, *Kit Kat & Lucy: The Country Cats Who Changed a City Girl's World*. She lives in southern Michigan with her husband and two highly evolved cats.

Hope Ellis-Ashburn is an award-winning author, dynamic educator, equestrian, and farmer. In addition to her bi-monthly column in *Hobby Farms* magazine, "From My Farm," over one hundred of her articles have appeared in twelve iconic equestrian publications such as *Horse Illustrated* magazine. She is also the author of two books and a riding journal. You can read more about Hope, her books, and her magazine articles on her website, RedHorseOnARedHill .PubsitePro.com.

Jan Epp graduated from the University of Wisconsin-Madison School of Nursing. She had a very successful forty-eight-year career in correctional health care, from which she recently retired as a regional vice president. She lives in Michigan with all her adopted animals, including four burros from the Bureau of Land Management—her "California Girls."

Glenda Ferguson (tgferguson@frontier.com) has contributed to *All God's Creatures*, *Chicken Soup for the Soul*, *Mules & More*, and *Sasee*. Her writing encouragement comes from the Writers Forum of Burton Kimble Farms Education Center and the ladies' prayer circle at her church. As an Indiana Landmarks volunteer, she conducts tours for two historical hotels and often visits The Stables, home of the trio of horses. Glenda and her husband, Tim, share an acre of land with Speckles the cat and a variety of wildlife visitors.

Tahlia Fischer's passion for saving horses and donkeys is rooted in her childhood—animals seemed to come to her ever since she could walk. She founded her equine rescue, All Seated in a Barn, a 501(c)(3) nonprofit, and it has given her the platform to make a difference and help change the horse industry. Outside the barn, she enjoys spending her time with her dogs and her family. She and her rescues can be found at www.AllSeatedInABarn.com.

Barbara Ellin Fox has spent her life training horses and riders. She weaves her extensive background with horses and their people into exciting stories about happily ever after. Since leaving her home on Long Island, New York, and living in the Southwest, Barbara adds a unique East meets West flavor to her writing. She is an equestrian blogger at TheRidingInstructor.net, where she shares encouragement and teaching tips with other instructors.

Peggy Frezon is a contributing editor at *Guideposts* magazine. She's the author of multiple books about the human-animal bond, including the bestseller *Mini Horse, Mighty Hope* (with Debbie Garcia-Bengochea), and a regular contributor to *All God's Creatures Daily Devotions*, *Pray a Word a Day*, and other devotionals. Peggy and her husband, Mike, rescue senior golden retrievers and share their home with goldens Ernest and Petey, and two rescue guinea pigs, Petunia and Marigold. Connect with Peggy at www.PeggyFrezon.com.

Susan Friedland writes about horses and the equestrian lifestyle on her award-winning blog *Saddle Seeks Horse*, where you will find her blog post "Kissing Spine Hope." Author of the books *Horses Adored and Men Endured* and *Strands of Hope: How to Grieve* *the Loss of a Horse*, Susan lives in Chicago and winters in Ocala, Florida. Connect with her and Tiz A Knight at SaddleSeeksHorse on Instagram or Facebook and at SaddleSeeksHorse.com.

Debbie Garcia-Bengochea is a former teacher and school principal. She is also a bestselling author, award-winning commercial artist and photographer, and the co-founder of Gentle Carousel Miniature Therapy Horses (www.GentleCarouselTherapyHorses .com). The 501(c)(3) nonprofit charity celebrated twenty-five years of service in 2022. Look for more information about the therapy horses in the book *Mini Horse, Mighty Hope*, an EQUUS Film and Arts Festival Literary Winner, and in *Gentle Carousel Miniature Therapy Horses Inspirational Deck and Guidebook*.

Jenny Lynn Keller is an award-winning writer whose Appalachian Mountain heritage infuses her writing with hope, humor, and a touch of Southern charm. Her beloved animal stories appear in Callie Smith Grant's compilations *The Horse of My Dreams*, *The Dog Who Came to Christmas*, and *The Cat in the Christmas Tree*. Read her devotions in *Guideposts' Walking in Grace*. Contact her at www.JennyLynnKeller.com.

After retiring from a career in marketing and public relations, **Chris Kent** (bruleridge@gmail.com) and her husband moved to a remote area of the Upper Peninsula of Michigan, where they live with their two quarter horses and a German Shorthair. Chris belongs to a group of North Woods writers and has been published in *Equus* magazine and in several volumes of *U.P. Reader*. She enjoys gardening, making maple syrup, beekeeping, traveling, horseback riding, and volunteering in the community. She finds inspiration from the woods and the water where she lives, and she enjoys sharing her love of nature and animals when children and grandchildren visit their north country retreat.

Andi Lehman freelances in diverse markets, writing nonfiction stories, articles, devotions, and grants, and she is also an editor and popular speaker (live and virtual) who enjoys working with children and their parents. Her education company, Life with Animals, teaches the wonder of all creatures and our responsibility to care for them. Her book *Saving Schmiddy* is the first in a conservation series for kids, and Andi is currently working on the second book for that series. To learn more about Andi's work with words and animals, visit AndiLehman.com.

Nicole M. Miller is a longtime Arabian horse owner and enthusiast who works in human resources by day and writes historical fiction by night. Her debut novel will be released by Revell in June 2024, a story that follows the eruption of World War II and the dramatic efforts to save the priceless Arabian horses of Poland. She lives near Vancouver, Washington, with her husband and two boys and a vast assortment of horses, dogs, cats, and chickens.

Dani Nichols is a writer, cowgirl, and mom of three from Central Oregon. Her debut book for children, *Buzz the Not-So-Brave*, about her quirky and skittish quarter horse, released in summer 2022 and is available for purchase on her website. Her work has won several writing contests and has been published in *Fathom*, *Oregon Humanities*, *Fallow Ink*, and others. To read more from Dani, check out www.WranglerDani.com and @BuzzTheNotSo Brave on Instagram.

Fay Odeh is a mother of eight, a grandmother of fourteen, a baker, and a restaurateur. She and her late husband, Steve, opened a family-style restaurant in southeastern Michigan many years ago, and Fay continues to run it today. She is especially known for the restaurant's cakes and pies that she bakes herself.

Jane Owen is a retired teacher and freelance writer whose short stories, feature articles, and devotional writings have appeared in works published by St. Martin's Press, Bethany House, Guidepost Books, and others. Recently, Grace Publishing House included a story about her beloved grandmother in *Grandma's Cookie Jar*.

She and her husband, Ron, have shared fifty-five years together, and their three grandchildren are "icing on the cake!" Contact her at ladyjaneut@aol.com.

Katherine Pasour is an author, teacher, farmer, speaker, and a life-long lover of horses. She blogs regularly at www.KatherinePasour.com with a focus on faith, wellness, and lessons that nature teaches. Katherine's book, *Honoring God with My Body: Journey to Wellness and a Healthy Lifestyle*, published in 2022, encourages lifestyle choices for a healthier and happier life. You can connect with Katherine on Facebook at Sheltered by an Angel's Wings and Instagram at KatherinePasourAuthor and on Twitter @KatherinePasour.

Carmen Peone is an award-winning author of young adult and contemporary Western romance. She lives with her husband in Northeast Washington and on the Colville Confederated Indian Reservation. With the love of history and the Western woman's lifestyle, she weaves threads of healing, hope, and horses into her stories. Connect with Carmen and sign up for her newsletter at CarmenPeone.com.

Kim Peterson and her husband go out of their way to be near horses—Thoroughbreds, draft horses, ponies, they love them all. A freelance writer and conference speaker, Kim proofreads and edits for a small publishing house and also mentors writers online for Taylor University. Her writing has appeared in various anthologies, including *Chicken Soup for the Caregiver's Soul*, *The Cat in the Christmas Tree*, and *Moments with Billy Graham*. Meet Kim at NatureWalkWithGod.WordPress.com/Welcome and encounter God's creation through her blog.

Kristi Ross (also known as Kristi Kjeldgaard) is a former American Quarter Horse Association clinician and successful horse trainer and coach. She is the mother of Mika and grandmother of Rossi, who both love horses. Kristi uses her life experiences with horses and people and her faith walk with God to heal hearts and transform lives through her in-person and online coaching, trainings, and books. Connect with her at www.KristiRoss.com and on her Facebook page at Kristi Ross Author.

Claudia Wolfe St. Clair is an artist, writer, retired art therapist, and *anam cara* from Toledo, Ohio. She is the mother of three and grandmother of six. She and the love of her life have restored the family home and gardens on Lake Erie. You can read more from Claudia in the Callie Smith Grant collections *The Horse of My Dreams*, *The Horse of My Heart*, *Second-Chance Dogs*, *Second-Chance Cats*, *The Dog Who Came to Christmas*, and *The Cat in the Christmas Tree*.

Karen Thurman was born on Long Island in 1952. She always said the love of horses was born inside of her. Through her hard work and perseverance, Karen has made a home for blind horses and a life worth living for herself.

Connie Webster has been a lover of animals since her earliest childhood. She enjoys life in rural Michigan, living on the farm where she grew up and raised her children. When she isn't riding the trails with her friends or exploring the countryside with her grandchildren, she adventures with her husband and tends her happy horses and her dogs.

About the Compiler

Callie Smith Grant enjoys animals of all kinds. She is the author of many published animal stories and several biographies. She is the compiler and editor of the award-winning anthologies *Second-Chance Cats* (awarded the Muse Medallion from Cat Writers' Association) and *Second-Chance Dogs* (awarded the Maxwell Medallion from Dog Writers Association of America). She is also the compiler and editor of *The Horse of My Dreams*, *The Horse of My Heart*, *The Dog Who Came to Christmas*, *The Dog at My Feet*, *The Dog Next Door*, *The Cat in My Lap*, *The Cat in the Window*, and *The Cat in the Christmas Tree*.

Acknowledgments

Many thanks to my editor and friend, Dr. Vicki Crumpton, for all the grace, kindness, and wisdom. She has given many animals their own second chances over the years.